The
Gospel
of
Luke

_____

Presented to

_____

Presented by

_____

Date

_____

Occasion

The Gospel of Luke
The Illustrated International Children's Bible®
Copyright © 2006 by Thomas Nelson, Inc

Illustrations and layout Copyright © 2006 Neely Publishing LLC.
Illustrations by Keith Neely and David Miles

International Children's Bible®
Copyright © 1986, 1988, 1999 by Tommy Nelson™ , a division of Thomas Nelson, Inc.
All Rights Reserved.

Permissions requests for the International Children's Bible® should be submitted in
writing in advance of use.
Contact: Tommy Nelson, PO Box 141000, Nashville, TN 37214

The preliminary research and development of the International Children's Bible® was
done by the World Bible Translation Center, Inc., Fort Worth, TX 76182

All Rights Reserved.
Printed in the United States of America

1 2 3 4 5 6 7 8 9 10 – 13 12 11 10 09 08 07 06

The Gospel of Luke

 The Illustrated
International Children's Bible®

Design and Illustration from
Neely Publishing LLC.

Individual contributors:
Keith R. Neely, David Miles, Roberta Neely,
Bridget Harlow and Thomas R. Zuber

A Division of Thomas Nelson Publishers
Since 1798

www.TommyNelson.com
a division of
Thomas Nelson, Inc.
www.thomasnelson.com

Introduction

Welcome! You've just picked up one of the most amazing books of all time, the Holy Bible. This book of the Bible, Luke, is presented in a way that has never been done before. Want to know how and why we've done it this way? Keep reading to find out!

Our Purpose
We did not want to create just another children's Bible story-book. In other words, we didn't want to have Bible pictures alongside words that are a retelling of God's Word, the Holy Scriptures. We wanted to draw attention to, magnify, and clarify the actual Word of God. In those words lies the power to change the lives of children and adults alike!

"God's word is alive and working." Hebrews 4:12

"But the word of the Lord will live forever." 1 Peter 1:25

In the same way that written illustrations or "word pictures" are used to help make an idea easy to understand and memorable, our visual illustrations will make the actual Word of God easier to understand than ever before.

The Illustrated International Children's Bible®
The International Children's Bible® was the first translation created especially for children. It has been illustrated in a frame-by-frame format style. These realistic images help illustrate the actual Scriptures . . . the events of the Bible. The format helps to carry the reader easily through each story like a visual movie. This not only makes the verses easier to understand, but also easier to memorize!

Not Against Us Is for Us 49 John answered, "Master, we saw someone using your name to force demons out of people. We told him to stop because he does not belong to our group." 50 Jesus said to him, "Don't stop him. If a person is not against you, then he is for you."

Luke 9:49-59

The men went into...

Actual Scriptures: Yes, that's right . . . the pages of this book are actual Bible verses. On some pages you'll see the characters speaking by the use of a dialog box. The action and setting of the scene is readily apparent by the backgrounds. What a great way to read and learn your Bible! Some of the verses are not a person speaking, so they will be in plain boxes. You might see some small "d's" in the text. These indicate a word that will have a definition in the dictionary found at the back of full ICB Bibles.

Old Testament quotations are shown in a separate treatment. They are in a parchment like background to represent that they are older words, almost like a treasured antique. They will usually have the book, chapter, and verse with them so you can know where they came from in the Old Testament.

5 "Tell the people of Jerusalem, 'Your king is coming to you. He is gentle and riding on a donkey. He is on the colt of a donkey.' "

Zechariah 9:9

12:7 'I . . . sacrifices.' Quotation from Hosea 6:6.
12:10 "Is it right . . . day?" It was against Jewish law to work on the Sabbath day.

30

Footnotes appear at the bottom of some pages. They are represented in the Bible verses by small "n's." They will let you know that there is a note at the bottom of the page that gives you a little more information about that word or phrase. Just more information that's helpful to know!

In some chapters and verses there will not be a lot of interaction between Bible characters, but you will see background scenery, maps, and other interesting treatments to help make your Bible reading more fun and helpful. Most Bible storybooks are just that . : . stories retold to make them easier to understand. Never before has actual Bible Scripture been illustrated in this form so that children and adults can immediately read and know what is going on in a certain verse—who was talking, what time of day it was, was it inside or out, who was there. We hope you enjoy reading this Bible and have fun learning along the way!

The Publishers

Look for these other titles...

and

Table of Contents

Chapter 1

Luke Writes About Jesus' Life....1
Zechariah and Elizabeth............1
The Virgin Mary.......................3
Mary's Visit...............................5
Mary Praises God.....................5
The Birth of John......................6
Zechariah Praises God..............7

Chapter 2

The Birth of Jesus.....................8
Some Shepherds Hear
About Jesus............................9
Jesus Is Presented
in the Temple.......................11
Simeon Sees Jesus...................11
Anna Sees Jesus......................11
Joseph and Mary
Return Home.......................12
Jesus as a Boy........................12

Chapter 3

The Preaching of John.............13
Jesus Is Baptized
by John.................................15

The Family History
of Jesus..................................16

Chapter 4

Jesus Is Tempted
by the Devil...........................17
Jesus Teaches the People........18
Jesus Removes
an Evil-Spirit..........................20
Jesus Heals Many People.........20

Chapter 5

Jesus' First Followers..............21
Jesus Heals a Sick Man...........23
Jesus Heals
a Paralyzed Man.....................24
Levi Follows Jesus...................25
Jesus Answers a Question.......26

Chapter 6

Jesus Is Lord
over the Sabbath....................26
Jesus Heals
a Man's Crippled Hand...........27
Jesus Chooses His Apostles.....28
Jesus Teaches and Heals.........29
Love Your Enemies..................29
Look at Yourselves..................30
Two Kinds of Fruit...................30
Two Kinds of People...............30

Chapter 7

Jesus Heals
a Soldier's Servant..................31

Jesus Brings a Man
Back to Life..............................32
John Asks a Question..............33
Simon the Pharisee................34

Chapter 8

The Group with Jesus..............36
A Story About
Planting Seed..........................37
Use What You Have................38
Jesus' True Family..................39
Jesus Stops a Storm................39
A Man with Demons
Inside Him..............................41
Jesus Gives Life to a Dead Girl
and Heals a Sick Woman.........42

Chapter 9

Jesus Sends Out
the Apostles............................45
Herod Is Confused
About Jesus............................46
More than 5,000
People Fed..............................46

Jesus Is the Christ..................47
Jesus with
Moses and Elijah....................48
Jesus Heals a Sick Boy............49
Jesus Talks About His Death...50
The Most Important Person.....50
Anyone Not Against Us
Is for Us..................................51
A Samaritan Town..................51
Following Jesus......................51

Chapter 10

Jesus Sends the 72 Men...........52
Jesus Warns Believers..............52
Satan Falls..............................53
Jesus Prays to the Father.........53
The Good Samaritan...............54
Mary and Martha....................55

Chapter 11

Jesus Teaches About Prayer.....56
Continue to Ask......................56
Jesus' Power Is from God.........57
The Empty Man......................58
People Who Are
Truly Blessed..........................58
Give Us Proof!........................58
Be a Light for the World..........59
Jesus Accuses the Pharisees....59
Jesus Talks to
Teachers of the Law................60

Chapter 12

Don't Be Like the Pharisees.....60
Fear Only God..........................61
Don't Be Ashamed of Jesus......61
Jesus Warns
Against Selfishness.................61

Don't Worry..............................62
Don't Trust in Money..............63
Always Be Ready....................63
Who Is
the Trusted Servant?...............63
Jesus Causes Division.............64
Understanding the Times........64
Settle Your Problems..............64

Chapter 13
Change Your Hearts................65
The Useless Tree.....................65
Jesus Heals on the Sabbath.....65
Stories of Mustard Seed
and Yeast................................67
The Narrow Door....................67
Jesus Will Die in Jerusalem.......68

Chapter 14
Is It Right to Heal
on the Sabbath?.....................69
Don't Make
Yourself Important.................69
You Will Be Rewarded.............70
A Story About
a Big Banquet........................70
You Must First Plan.................71
Don't Lose Your Influence.......72

Chapter 15
A Lost Sheep
and a Lost Coin.....................72
The Son Who Left Home..........73

Chapter 16
True Wealth.............................75
God's Law Cannot
Be Changed...........................76

Divorce and Remarriage..........76
The Rich Man and Lazarus.......77

Chapter 17
Sin and Forgiveness................78
How Big Is Your Faith?.............78
Be Good Servants....................78
Be Thankful.............................79
God's Kingdom
Is Within You...........................79
When Jesus Comes Again........80

Chapter 18
God Will Answer
His People................................81
Being Right with God..............81
Who Will Enter
God's Kingdom?......................82
A Rich Man's Question............83
Who Can Be Saved?................83
Jesus Will Rise from Death.......84
Jesus Heals a Blind Man..........84

Chapter 19
Zacchaeus.............................85

A Story About
Three Servants........................86

Jesus Enters Jerusalem
as a King................................88

Jesus Cries for Jerusalem.........89
Jesus Goes to the Temple........90

Chapter 20

The Leaders Question Jesus....90
God Sends His Son..................91
The Leaders Try
to Trap Jesus..........................92
Sadducees Try
to Trick Jesus.........................93
Is the Christ
the Son of David?...................93
Jesus Accuses the Leaders.......93

Chapter 21

True Giving............................94
The Temple
Will Be Destroyed..................94

Jerusalem
Will Be Destroyed..................95
Don't Fear..............................95
My Words Will Live Forever......96
Be Ready All the Time.............96

Chapter 22

Plans to Kill Jesus...................96
Preparation of the
Passover Meal.........................97
The Lord's Supper...................98
Who Will Turn
Against Jesus?.........................99
Be Like a Servant....................99
Don't Lose Your Faith............100
Be Ready for Trouble.............100
Jesus Prays Alone..................100
Jesus Is Arrested...................101
Peter Says He Doesn't
Know Jesus...........................102
The People Laugh at Jesus.....103
Jesus Before the Leaders.......103

Chapter 23

Governor Pilate
Questions Jesus....................104
Pilate Sends Jesus to Herod...104
Jesus Must Die......................105
Jesus Is Killed on a Cross.......107
Jesus Dies.............................109
Joseph of Arimathea.............110

Chapter 24

Jesus Rises from Death.........111
On the Road to Emmaus........112
Jesus Appears
to His Followers....................114
Jesus Goes Back to Heaven....115

The Gospel of Luke

Luke Writes About Jesus' Life

Luke Chapter 1

1 To Theophilus:
Many have tried to give a history of the things that happened among us. 2 They have written the same things that we learned from others—the people who saw those things from the beginning and served God by telling people his message. 3 I myself studied everything carefully from the beginning, your Excellency." I thought I should write it out for you. So I put it in order in a book. 4 I write these things so that you can know that what you have been taught is true.

Zechariah and Elizabeth

5 During the time Herod ruled Judea, there was a priest named Zechariah. He belonged to Abijah's group." Zechariah's wife came from the family of Aaron. Her name was Elizabeth. 6 Zechariah and Elizabeth truly did what God said was good. They did everything the Lord commanded and told people to do. They were without fault in keeping his law. 7 But Zechariah and Elizabeth had no children. Elizabeth could not have a baby; and both of them were very old.

8 Zechariah was serving as a priest before God for his group. It was his group's time to serve. 9 According to the custom of the priests, he was chosen to go into the Temple of the Lord and burn incense.

10 There were a great many people outside praying at the time the incense was offered.

1:3 Excellency This word was used to show respect to an important person like a king or ruler. **1:5 Abijah's group** The Jewish priests were divided into 24 groups. See 1 Chronicles 24.

11 Then, on the right side of the incense table, an angel of the Lord came and stood before Zechariah. 12 When he saw the angel, Zechariah was confused and frightened. 13 But the angel said to him,

"Zechariah, don't be afraid. Your prayer has been heard by God. Your wife, Elizabeth, will give birth to a son. You will name him John. 14 You will be very happy. Many people will be happy because of his birth. 15 John will be a great man for the Lord. He will never drink wine or beer. Even at the time John is born, he will be filled with the Holy Spirit.d 16 He will help many people of Israel return to the Lord their God. 17 He himself will go first before the Lord. John will be powerful in spirit like Elijah. He will make peace between fathers and their children. He will bring those who are not obeying God back to the right way of thinking. He will make people ready for the coming of the Lord."

18 Zechariah said to the angel,

"How can I know that what you say is true? I am an old man, and my wife is old, too."

19 The angel answered him,

"I am Gabriel. I stand before God. God sent me to talk to you and to tell you this good news. 20 Now, listen! You will not be able to talk until the day these things happen. You will lose your speech because you did not believe what I told you. But these things will really happen."

21 Outside, the people were still waiting for Zechariah. They were surprised that he was staying so long in the Temple. 22 Then Zechariah came outside, but he could not speak to them. So they knew that he had seen a vision in the Temple. Zechariah could not speak. He could only make signs to them.

23 When his time of service as a priest was finished, he went home.
24 Later, Zechariah's wife, Elizabeth, became pregnant. She did not go out of her house for five months. Elizabeth said,

25 "Look what the Lord has done for me! My people were ashamed[n] of me, but now the Lord has taken away that shame."

The Virgin Mary

26-27 During Elizabeth's sixth month of pregnancy, God sent the angel Gabriel to a virgin[d] who lived in Nazareth, a town in Galilee. She was engaged to marry a man named Joseph from the family of David. Her name was Mary.

28 The angel came to her and said,

29 But Mary was very confused by what the angel said. Mary wondered,

"Greetings! The Lord has blessed you and is with you."

"What does this mean?"

1:25 ashamed The Jews thought it was a disgrace for women not to have children.

3

30 The angel said to her,

"Don't be afraid, Mary, because God is pleased with you. 31 Listen! You will become pregnant. You will give birth to a son, and you will name him Jesus. 32 He will be great, and people will call him the Son of the Most High. The Lord God will give him the throne of King David, his ancestor. 33 He will rule over the people of Jacob forever. His kingdom will never end."

34 Mary said to the angel,

"How will this happen? I am a virgin!"

35 The angel said to Mary,

"The Holy Spirit[d] will come upon you, and the power of the Most High will cover you. The baby will be holy. He will be called the Son of God. 36 Now listen! Elizabeth, your relative, is very old. But she is also pregnant with a son. Everyone thought she could not have a baby, but she has been pregnant for six months. 37 God can do everything!"

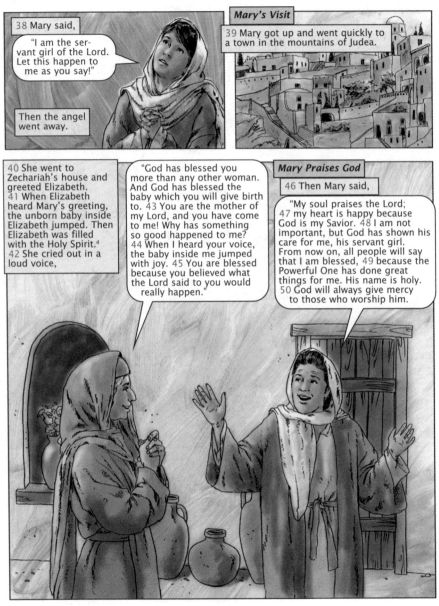

38 Mary said,

"I am the servant girl of the Lord. Let this happen to me as you say!"

Then the angel went away.

Mary's Visit

39 Mary got up and went quickly to a town in the mountains of Judea.

40 She went to Zechariah's house and greeted Elizabeth. 41 When Elizabeth heard Mary's greeting, the unborn baby inside Elizabeth jumped. Then Elizabeth was filled with the Holy Spirit.[d] 42 She cried out in a loud voice,

"God has blessed you more than any other woman. And God has blessed the baby which you will give birth to. 43 You are the mother of my Lord, and you have come to me! Why has something so good happened to me? 44 When I heard your voice, the baby inside me jumped with joy. 45 You are blessed because you believed what the Lord said to you would really happen."

Mary Praises God

46 Then Mary said,

"My soul praises the Lord; 47 my heart is happy because God is my Savior. 48 I am not important, but God has shown his care for me, his servant girl. From now on, all people will say that I am blessed, 49 because the Powerful One has done great things for me. His name is holy. 50 God will always give mercy to those who worship him.

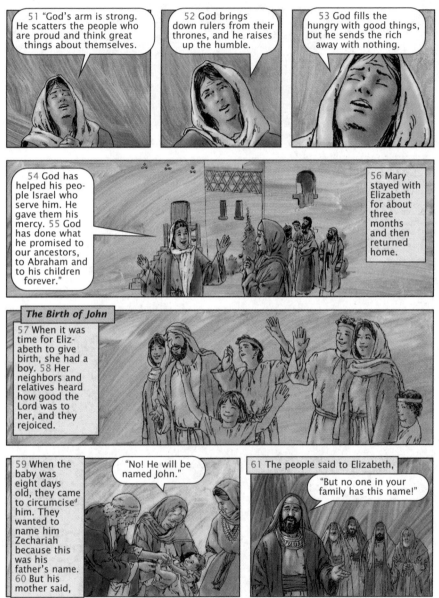

51 "God's arm is strong. He scatters the people who are proud and think great things about themselves.

52 God brings down rulers from their thrones, and he raises up the humble.

53 God fills the hungry with good things, but he sends the rich away with nothing.

54 God has helped his people Israel who serve him. He gave them his mercy. 55 God has done what he promised to our ancestors, to Abraham and to his children forever."

56 Mary stayed with Elizabeth for about three months and then returned home.

The Birth of John

57 When it was time for Elizabeth to give birth, she had a boy. 58 Her neighbors and relatives heard how good the Lord was to her, and they rejoiced.

59 When the baby was eight days old, they came to circumcise[d] him. They wanted to name him Zechariah because this was his father's name. 60 But his mother said,

"No! He will be named John."

61 The people said to Elizabeth,

"But no one in your family has this name!"

62 Then they made signs to his father, "What would you like to name him?" 63 Zechariah asked for something to write on. Then he wrote, "His name is John." Everyone was surprised. 64 Then Zechariah could talk again. He began to praise God.

"What will this child be?"

65 And all their neighbors became alarmed. In all the mountains of Judea people continued talking about all these things. 66 The people who heard about these things wondered about them. They thought,

They said this because the Lord was with him.

Zechariah Praises God

67 Then Zechariah, John's father, was filled with the Holy Spirit.[d] He told the people what would happen:

68 "Let us thank the Lord, the God of Israel. God has come to help his people and has given them freedom. 69 God has given us a powerful Savior from the family of God's servant David. 70 God said that he would do this. He said it through his holy prophets[d] who lived long ago. 71 God will save us from our enemies and from the power of all those who hate us. 72 God said he would give mercy to our ancestors. And he remembered his holy promise. 73 God promised

Abraham, our father, 74 that he would free us from the power of our enemies, so that we could serve him without fear. 75 We will be righteous and holy before God as long as we live. 76 "Now you, child, will be called a prophet of the Most High God. You will go first before the Lord to prepare the people for his coming. 77 You will make his people know that they will be saved. They will be saved by having their sins forgiven. 78 With the loving mercy of our God, a new day from heaven will shine upon us. 79 God will help those who live in darkness, in the fear of death. He will guide us into the path that goes toward peace."

80 And so the child grew up and became strong in spirit. John lived away from other people until the time when he came out to preach to Israel.

Chapter

2

The Birth of Jesus

1 At that time, Augustus Caesar[d] sent an order to all people in the countries that were under Roman rule. The order said that they must list their names in a register. 2 This was the first registration[n] taken while Quirinius was governor of Syria. 3 And everyone went to their own towns to be registered.

4 So Joseph left Nazareth, a town in Galilee. He went to the town of Bethlehem in Judea. This town was known as the town of David. Joseph went there because he was from the family of David. 5 Joseph registered with Mary because she was engaged to marry him. (Mary was now pregnant.)

6 While Joseph and Mary were in Bethlehem, the time came for her to have the baby.

7 She gave birth to her first son.

2:2 registration Census. A counting of all the people and the things they own.

There were no rooms left in the inn. So she wrapped the baby with cloths and laid him in a box where animals are fed.

Some Shepherds Hear About Jesus

8 That night, some shepherds were in the fields nearby watching their sheep. 9 An angel of the Lord stood before them. The glory of the Lord was shining around them, and suddenly they became very frightened. 10 The angel said to them,

"Don't be afraid, because I am bringing you some good news. It will be a joy to all the people. 11 Today your Savior was born in David's town. He is Christ,[d] the Lord. 12 This is how you will know him: You will find a baby wrapped in cloths and lying in a feeding box."

2:14 and . . . God Some Greek copies read "and on earth let there be peace and goodwill among people."

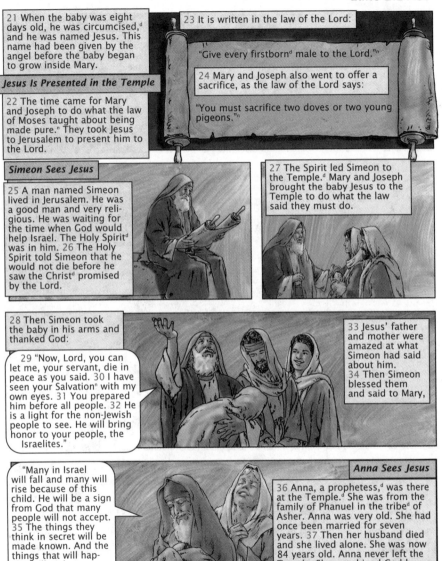

21 When the baby was eight days old, he was circumcised,[d] and he was named Jesus. This name had been given by the angel before the baby began to grow inside Mary.

Jesus Is Presented in the Temple

22 The time came for Mary and Joseph to do what the law of Moses taught about being made pure.[n] They took Jesus to Jerusalem to present him to the Lord.

23 It is written in the law of the Lord:

"Give every firstborn[d] male to the Lord."[n]

24 Mary and Joseph also went to offer a sacrifice, as the law of the Lord says:

"You must sacrifice two doves or two young pigeons."[n]

Simeon Sees Jesus

25 A man named Simeon lived in Jerusalem. He was a good man and very religious. He was waiting for the time when God would help Israel. The Holy Spirit[d] was in him. 26 The Holy Spirit told Simeon that he would not die before he saw the Christ[d] promised by the Lord.

27 The Spirit led Simeon to the Temple.[d] Mary and Joseph brought the baby Jesus to the Temple to do what the law said they must do.

28 Then Simeon took the baby in his arms and thanked God:

29 "Now, Lord, you can let me, your servant, die in peace as you said. 30 I have seen your Salvation[n] with my own eyes. 31 You prepared him before all people. 32 He is a light for the non-Jewish people to see. He will bring honor to your people, the Israelites."

33 Jesus' father and mother were amazed at what Simeon had said about him. 34 Then Simeon blessed them and said to Mary,

"Many in Israel will fall and many will rise because of this child. He will be a sign from God that many people will not accept. 35 The things they think in secret will be made known. And the things that will happen will make your heart sad, too."

Anna Sees Jesus

36 Anna, a prophetess,[d] was there at the Temple.[d] She was from the family of Phanuel in the tribe[d] of Asher. Anna was very old. She had once been married for seven years. 37 Then her husband died and she lived alone. She was now 84 years old. Anna never left the Temple. She worshiped God by going without food and praying day and night.

2:22 **pure** The law of Moses said that 40 days after a Jewish woman gave birth to a baby, she must be cleansed by a ceremony at the Temple. Read Leviticus 12:2-8.
2:23 **"Give . . . Lord."** Quotation from Exodus 13:2.
2:24 **"You . . . pigeons."** Quotation from Leviticus 12:8.
2:30 **Salvation** Simeon was talking about Jesus. The name Jesus means "salvation." 11

Luke 2:38-48

38 She was standing there at that time, thanking God. She talked about Jesus to all who were waiting for God to free Jerusalem.

Joseph and Mary Return Home

39 Joseph and Mary finished doing everything that the law of the Lord commanded. Then they went home to Nazareth, their own town in Galilee. 40 The little child began to grow up. He became stronger and wiser, and God's blessings were with him.

Jesus as a Boy

41 Every year Jesus' parents went to Jerusalem for the Passover[d] Feast. 42 When Jesus was 12 years old, they went to the feast as they always did. 43 When the feast days were over, they went home. The boy Jesus stayed behind in Jerusalem, but his parents did not know it. 44 Joseph and Mary traveled for a whole day. They thought that Jesus was with them in the group. Then they began to look for him among their family and friends, 45 but they did not find him. So they went back to Jerusalem to look for him there.

46 After three days they found him. Jesus was sitting in the Temple[d] with the religious teachers, listening to them and asking them questions. 47 All who heard him were amazed at his understanding and wise answers. 48 When Jesus' parents saw him, they were amazed.

His mother said to him,

"Son, why did you do this to us? Your father and I were very worried about you. We have been looking for you."

49 Jesus asked,

"Why did you have to look for me? You should have known that I must be where my Father's work is!"

50 But they did not understand the meaning of what he said.
51 Jesus went with them to Nazareth and obeyed them. His mother was still thinking about all that had happened.

52 Jesus continued to learn more and more and to grow physically. People liked him, and he pleased God.

The Preaching of John

Chapter 3

1 It was the fifteenth year of the rule of Tiberius Caesar.[d] These men were under Caesar: Pontius Pilate was the ruler of Judea. Herod was the ruler of Galilee. Philip, Herod's brother, was the ruler of Iturea and Trachonitis. And Lysanias was the ruler of Abilene. 2 Annas and Caiaphas were the high priests. At this time, a command from God came to John son of Zechariah. John was living in the desert. 3 He went all over the area around the Jordan River and preached to the people. He preached a baptism of changed hearts and lives for the forgiveness of their sins. 4 As it is written in the book of Isaiah the prophet:[d]

"This is a voice of a man who calls out in the desert: 'Prepare the way for the Lord. Make the road straight for him. 5 Every valley should be filled in. Every mountain and hill should be made flat. Roads with turns should be made straight, and rough roads should be made smooth. 6 And all people will know about the salvation of God!' "

Isaiah 40:3-5

13

7 Crowds of people came to be baptized by John. He said to them,

"You poisonous snakes! Who warned you to run away from God's anger that is coming? 8 You must do the things that will show that you really have changed your hearts. Don't say, 'Abraham is our father.' I tell you that God can make children for Abraham from these rocks here. 9 The ax is now ready to cut down the trees. Every tree that does not produce good fruit will be cut down and thrown into the fire."[n]

10 The people asked John,

"What should we do?...

11 John answered,

"If you have two shirts, share with the person who does not have one.

If you have food, share that too."

3:9 The ax . . . fire. This means that God is ready to punish his people who do not obey him.

12 Even tax collectors came to John to be baptized. They said to John,

"Teacher, what should we do?"

13 John said to them,

"Don't take more taxes from people than you have been ordered to take."

14 The soldiers asked John,

"What about us? What should we do?"

John said to them,

"Don't force people to give you money. Don't lie about them. Be satisfied with the pay you get."

15 All the people were hoping for the Christ[d] to come, and they wondered about John. They thought, "Maybe he is the Christ." 16 John answered everyone,

"I baptize you with water, but there is one coming later who can do more than I can. I am not good enough to untie his sandals.

He will baptize you with the Holy Spirit[d] and with fire. 17 He will come ready to clean the grain. He will separate the good grain from the chaff.[d] He will put the good part of the grain into his barn. Then he will burn the chaff with a fire that cannot be put out."[n]

18 And John continued to preach the Good News,[d] saying many other things to encourage the people.

19 But John spoke against Herod, the governor, because of his sin with Herodias, the wife of Herod's brother. John also criticized Herod for the many other evil things Herod did. 20 So Herod did another evil thing: He put John in prison.

Jesus Is Baptized by John

21 When all the people were being baptized by John, Jesus also was baptized. While Jesus was praying,

3:17 He will . . . out. This means that Jesus will come to separate the good people from the bad people, saving the good and punishing the bad.

15

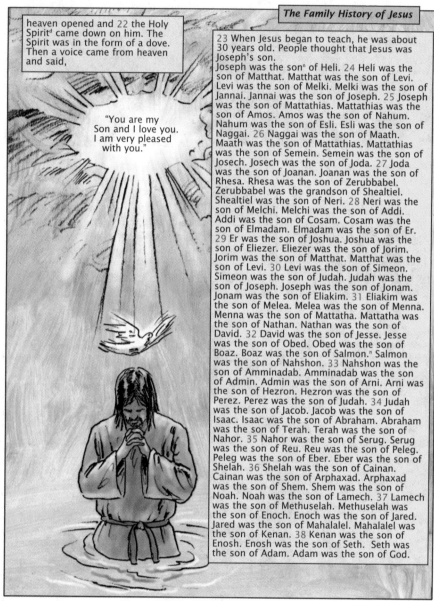

The Family History of Jesus

heaven opened and 22 the Holy Spirit[d] came down on him. The Spirit was in the form of a dove. Then a voice came from heaven and said,

"You are my Son and I love you. I am very pleased with you."

23 When Jesus began to teach, he was about 30 years old. People thought that Jesus was Joseph's son.

Joseph was the son[n] of Heli. 24 Heli was the son of Matthat. Matthat was the son of Levi. Levi was the son of Melchi. Melchi was the son of Jannai. Jannai was the son of Joseph. 25 Joseph was the son of Mattathias. Mattathias was the son of Amos. Amos was the son of Nahum. Nahum was the son of Esli. Esli was the son of Naggai. 26 Naggai was the son of Maath. Maath was the son of Mattathias. Mattathias was the son of Semein. Semein was the son of Josech. Josech was the son of Joda. 27 Joda was the son of Joanan. Joanan was the son of Rhesa. Rhesa was the son of Zerubbabel. Zerubbabel was the grandson of Shealtiel. Shealtiel was the son of Neri. 28 Neri was the son of Melchi. Melchi was the son of Addi. Addi was the son of Cosam. Cosam was the son of Elmadam. Elmadam was the son of Er. 29 Er was the son of Joshua. Joshua was the son of Eliezer. Eliezer was the son of Jorim. Jorim was the son of Matthat. Matthat was the son of Levi. 30 Levi was the son of Simeon. Simeon was the son of Judah. Judah was the son of Joseph. Joseph was the son of Jonam. Jonam was the son of Eliakim. 31 Eliakim was the son of Melea. Melea was the son of Menna. Menna was the son of Mattatha. Mattatha was the son of Nathan. Nathan was the son of David. 32 David was the son of Jesse. Jesse was the son of Obed. Obed was the son of Boaz. Boaz was the son of Salmon.[n] Salmon was the son of Nahshon. 33 Nahshon was the son of Amminadab. Amminadab was the son of Admin. Admin was the son of Arni. Arni was the son of Hezron. Hezron was the son of Perez. Perez was the son of Judah. 34 Judah was the son of Jacob. Jacob was the son of Isaac. Isaac was the son of Abraham. Abraham was the son of Terah. Terah was the son of Nahor. 35 Nahor was the son of Serug. Serug was the son of Reu. Reu was the son of Peleg. Peleg was the son of Eber. Eber was the son of Shelah. 36 Shelah was the son of Cainan. Cainan was the son of Arphaxad. Arphaxad was the son of Shem. Shem was the son of Noah. Noah was the son of Lamech. 37 Lamech was the son of Methuselah. Methuselah was the son of Enoch. Enoch was the son of Jared. Jared was the son of Mahalalel. Mahalalel was the son of Kenan. 38 Kenan was the son of Enosh. Enosh was the son of Seth. Seth was the son of Adam. Adam was the son of God.

3:23 son "Son" in Jewish lists of ancestors can sometimes mean grandson or more distant relative.
3:32 Salmon Some Greek copies read "Sala."

Chapter 4

Jesus Is Tempted by the Devil

1 Jesus, filled with the Holy Spirit,[d] returned from the Jordan River. The Spirit led Jesus into the desert 2 where the devil tempted Jesus for 40 days. Jesus ate nothing during that time. When those days were ended, he was very hungry. 3 The devil said to Jesus,

"If you are the Son of God, tell this rock to become bread."

4 Jesus answered,

"It is written in the Scriptures:[d] 'A person does not live only by eating bread.' "[n]

5 Then the devil took Jesus and showed him all the kingdoms of the world in a moment of time.

6 The devil said to Jesus,

"I will give you all these kingdoms and all their power and glory. It has all been given to me, and I can give it to anyone I wish. 7 If you worship me, all will be yours."

8 Jesus answered,

"It is written in the Scriptures: 'You must worship the Lord your God. Serve only him!' "[n]

9 Then the devil led Jesus to Jerusalem and put him on a high place of the Temple.[d]

4:4 'A person . . . bread.' Quotation from Deuteronomy 8:3.
4:8 'You . . . him!' Quotation from Deuteronomy 6:13.

Luke 4:10-19

He said to Jesus,

"If you are the Son of God, jump off! 10 It is written in the Scriptures:

'He has put his angels in charge of you. They will watch over you.'
Psalm 91:11
11 'They will catch you with their hands. And you will not hit your foot on a rock.' "
Psalm 91:12

12 Jesus answered,

"But it also says in the Scriptures: 'Do not test the Lord your God.' "[n]

13 After the devil had tempted Jesus in every way, he went away to wait until a better time.

Jesus Teaches the People

14 Jesus went back to Galilee with the power of the Holy Spirit.[d] Stories about Jesus spread all through the area. 15 He began to teach in the synagogues,[d] and all the people praised him.

16 Jesus traveled to Nazareth, where he had grown up. On the Sabbath[d] day he went to the synagogue as he always did. Jesus stood up to read. 17 The book of Isaiah the prophet[d] was given to him. He opened the book and found the place where this is written:

18 "The Spirit of the Lord is in me. This is because God chose me to tell the Good News[d] to the poor. God sent me to tell the prisoners of sin that they are free, and to tell the blind that they can see again.
Isaiah 61:1
God sent me to free those who have been treated unfairly,
Isaiah 58:6
19 and to announce the time when the Lord will show kindness to his people."
Isaiah 61:2

4:12 'Do . . . God.' Quotation from Deuteronomy 6:16.

18

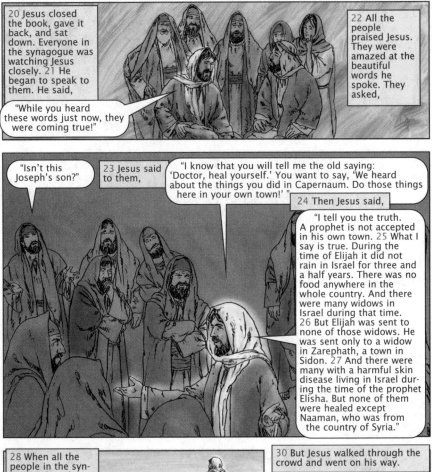

20 Jesus closed the book, gave it back, and sat down. Everyone in the synagogue was watching Jesus closely. 21 He began to speak to them. He said,

"While you heard these words just now, they were coming true!"

22 All the people praised Jesus. They were amazed at the beautiful words he spoke. They asked,

"Isn't this Joseph's son?"

23 Jesus said to them,

"I know that you will tell me the old saying: 'Doctor, heal yourself.' You want to say, 'We heard about the things you did in Capernaum. Do those things here in your own town!' "

24 Then Jesus said,

"I tell you the truth. A prophet is not accepted in his own town. 25 What I say is true. During the time of Elijah it did not rain in Israel for three and a half years. There was no food anywhere in the whole country. And there were many widows in Israel during that time. 26 But Elijah was sent to none of those widows. He was sent only to a widow in Zarephath, a town in Sidon. 27 And there were many with a harmful skin disease living in Israel during the time of the prophet Elisha. But none of them were healed except Naaman, who was from the country of Syria."

28 When all the people in the synagogue heard these things, they became very angry. 29 They got up and forced Jesus out of town. The town was built on a hill. They took Jesus to the edge of the hill and wanted to throw him off.

30 But Jesus walked through the crowd and went on his way.

19

Luke 4:31-39

Jesus Removes an Evil Spirit

31 Jesus went to Capernaum, a city in Galilee. On the Sabbath[d] day, Jesus taught the people. 32 They were amazed at his teaching, because he spoke with authority. 33 In the synagogue[d] there was a man who had an evil spirit from the devil inside him.

The man shouted in a loud voice,

34 "Jesus of Nazareth! What do you want with us? Did you come here to destroy us? I know who you are—God's Holy One!"

35 But Jesus warned the evil spirit to stop. He said,

"Be quiet! Come out of the man!"

The evil spirit threw the man down to the ground before all the people. Then the evil spirit left the man and did not hurt him.

36 The people were amazed. They said to each other,

"What does this mean? With authority and power he commands evil spirits, and they come out."

37 And so the news about Jesus spread to every place in the whole area.

Jesus Heals Many People

38 Jesus left the synagogue[d] and went to Simon's[n] house. Simon's mother-in-law was very sick with a high fever. They asked Jesus to do something to help her. 39 He stood very close to her and commanded the fever to leave. It left her immediately, and she got up and began serving them.

4:38 **Simon** Simon's other name was Peter.

40 When the sun went down, the people brought their sick to Jesus. They had many different diseases. Jesus put his hands on each sick person and healed every one of them. 41 Demons[d] came out of many people. The demons would shout,

"You are the Son of God."

But Jesus gave a strong command for the demons not to speak. They knew Jesus was the Christ.[d]

42 At daybreak, Jesus went to a place to be alone, but the people looked for him. When they found him, they tried to keep him from leaving. 43 But Jesus said to them,

"I must tell the Good News[d] about God's kingdom to other towns, too. This is why I was sent."

44 Then Jesus kept on preaching in the synagogues[d] of Judea.[n]

Chapter 5

Jesus' First Followers

1 One day Jesus was standing beside Lake Galilee. Many people were pressing all around him. They wanted to hear the word of God. 2 Jesus saw two boats at the shore of the lake. The fishermen had left them and were washing their nets.

4:44 Judea Some Greek copies read "Galilee."

21

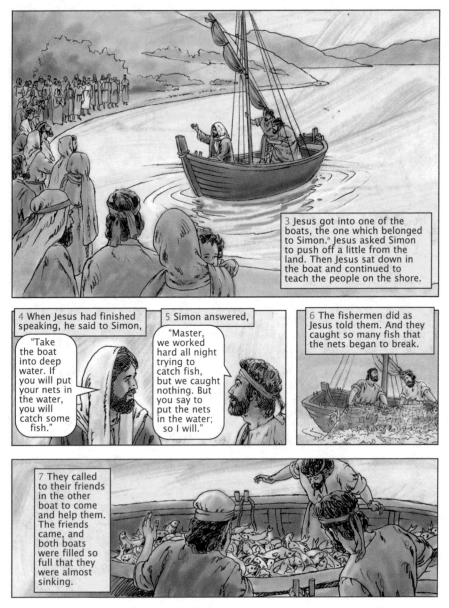

3 Jesus got into one of the boats, the one which belonged to Simon.* Jesus asked Simon to push off a little from the land. Then Jesus sat down in the boat and continued to teach the people on the shore.

4 When Jesus had finished speaking, he said to Simon,

"Take the boat into deep water. If you will put your nets in the water, you will catch some fish."

5 Simon answered,

"Master, we worked hard all night trying to catch fish, but we caught nothing. But you say to put the nets in the water; so I will."

6 The fishermen did as Jesus told them. And they caught so many fish that the nets began to break.

7 They called to their friends in the other boat to come and help them. The friends came, and both boats were filled so full that they were almost sinking.

5:3 Simon Simon's other name was Peter.

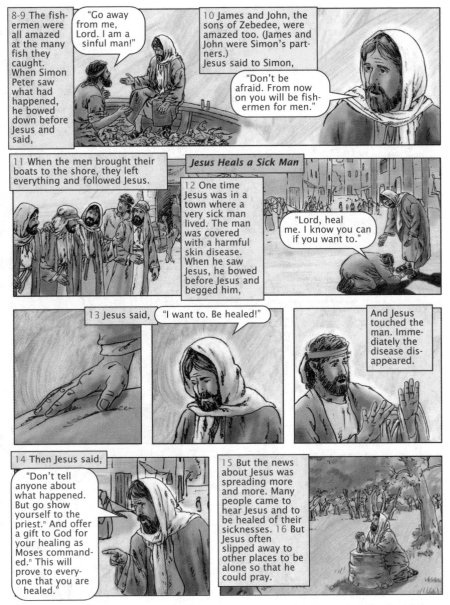

8-9 The fishermen were all amazed at the many fish they caught. When Simon Peter saw what had happened, he bowed down before Jesus and said,

"Go away from me, Lord. I am a sinful man!"

10 James and John, the sons of Zebedee, were amazed too. (James and John were Simon's partners.) Jesus said to Simon,

"Don't be afraid. From now on you will be fishermen for men."

11 When the men brought their boats to the shore, they left everything and followed Jesus.

Jesus Heals a Sick Man

12 One time Jesus was in a town where a very sick man lived. The man was covered with a harmful skin disease. When he saw Jesus, he bowed before Jesus and begged him,

"Lord, heal me. I know you can if you want to."

13 Jesus said, "I want to. Be healed!"

And Jesus touched the man. Immediately the disease disappeared.

14 Then Jesus said,

"Don't tell anyone about what happened. But go show yourself to the priest." And offer a gift to God for your healing as Moses commanded." This will prove to everyone that you are healed."

15 But the news about Jesus was spreading more and more. Many people came to hear Jesus and to be healed of their sicknesses. 16 But Jesus often slipped away to other places to be alone so that he could pray.

5:14 show . . . priest The law of Moses said a priest must say when a Jew with a harmful skin disease was well. **5:14 Moses commanded** Read about this in Leviticus 14:1-32.

23

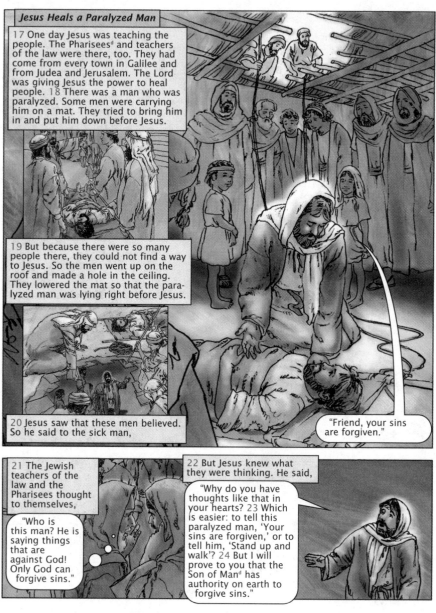

Jesus Heals a Paralyzed Man

17 One day Jesus was teaching the people. The Pharisees[d] and teachers of the law were there, too. They had come from every town in Galilee and from Judea and Jerusalem. The Lord was giving Jesus the power to heal people. 18 There was a man who was paralyzed. Some men were carrying him on a mat. They tried to bring him in and put him down before Jesus.

19 But because there were so many people there, they could not find a way to Jesus. So the men went up on the roof and made a hole in the ceiling. They lowered the mat so that the paralyzed man was lying right before Jesus.

20 Jesus saw that these men believed. So he said to the sick man,

"Friend, your sins are forgiven."

21 The Jewish teachers of the law and the Pharisees thought to themselves,

"Who is this man? He is saying things that are against God! Only God can forgive sins."

22 But Jesus knew what they were thinking. He said,

"Why do you have thoughts like that in your hearts? 23 Which is easier: to tell this paralyzed man, 'Your sins are forgiven,' or to tell him, 'Stand up and walk'? 24 But I will prove to you that the Son of Man[d] has authority on earth to forgive sins."

So Jesus said to the paralyzed man,

"I tell you, stand up! Take your mat and go home."

25 Then the man stood up before the people there. He picked up his mat and went home, praising God.

26 All the people were fully amazed and began to praise God.

They were filled with much respect and said,

"Today we have seen amazing things!"

Levi Follows Jesus

27 After this, Jesus went out and saw a tax collector named Levi sitting in the tax office. Jesus said to him,

"Follow me!"

28 Levi got up, left everything, and followed Jesus.

29 Then Levi gave a big dinner for Jesus. The dinner was at Levi's house. At the table there were many tax collectors and other people, too.

30 But the Pharisees[d] and the men who taught the law for the Pharisees began to complain to the followers of Jesus. They said,

"Why do you eat and drink with tax collectors and 'sinners'?"

31 Jesus answered them,

"Healthy people don't need a doctor. It is the sick who need a doctor. 32 I have not come to invite good people. I have come to invite sinners to change their hearts and lives!"

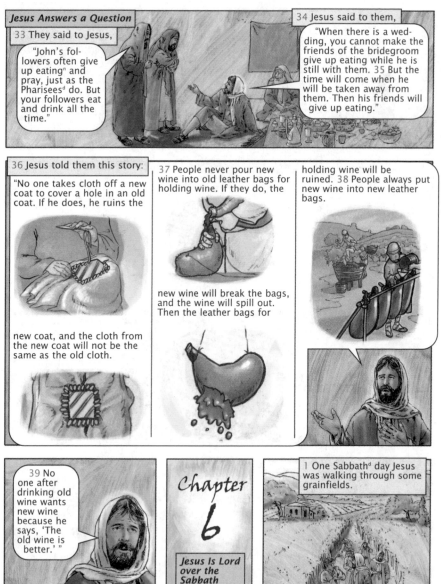

Jesus Answers a Question

33 They said to Jesus,

"John's followers often give up eating[n] and pray, just as the Pharisees[d] do. But your followers eat and drink all the time."

34 Jesus said to them,

"When there is a wedding, you cannot make the friends of the bridegroom give up eating while he is still with them. 35 But the time will come when he will be taken away from them. Then his friends will give up eating."

36 Jesus told them this story:

"No one takes cloth off a new coat to cover a hole in an old coat. If he does, he ruins the new coat, and the cloth from the new coat will not be the same as the old cloth.

37 People never pour new wine into old leather bags for holding wine. If they do, the new wine will break the bags, and the wine will spill out. Then the leather bags for holding wine will be ruined. 38 People always put new wine into new leather bags.

39 No one after drinking old wine wants new wine because he says, 'The old wine is better.' "

Chapter

6

Jesus Is Lord over the Sabbath

1 One Sabbath[d] day Jesus was walking through some grainfields.

5:33 give up eating This is called "fasting." The people would give up eating for a special time of prayer and worship to God. It was also done to show sadness.

His followers picked the heads of grain, rubbed them in their hands, and ate them.

2 Some Pharisees[d] said,

"Why are you doing that? It is against the law of Moses to do that on the Sabbath day."

3 Jesus answered,

"Haven't you read about what David did when he and those with him were hungry? 4 David went into God's house. He took the bread that was made holy for God and ate it. And he gave some of the bread to the people with him. This was against the law of Moses. It says that only priests can eat that bread."

5 Then Jesus said to the Pharisees,

"The Son of Man[d] is Lord of the Sabbath day."

Jesus Heals a Man's Crippled Hand

6 On another Sabbath[d] day Jesus went into the synagogue[d] and was teaching. A man with a crippled right hand was there. 7 The teachers of the law and the Pharisees[d] were watching to see if Jesus would heal on the Sabbath day. They wanted to see Jesus do something wrong so that they could accuse him. 8 But he knew what they were thinking.

He said to the man with the crippled hand,

"Get up and stand before these people."

The man got up and stood there. 9 Then Jesus said to them,

"I ask you, which is it right to do on the Sabbath day: to do good, or to do evil? Is it right to save a life or to destroy one?"

10 Jesus looked around at all of them. He said to the man,

"Let me see your hand."

The man stretched out his hand,

and it was completely healed.

11 The Pharisees and the teachers of the law became very angry. They said to each other,

"What can we do to Jesus?"

Jesus Chooses His Apostles

12 At that time Jesus went off to a mountain to pray. He stayed there all night, praying to God. 13 The next morning, Jesus called his followers to him. He chose 12 of them, whom he named "apostles."[d] They were

14 Simon (Jesus named him Peter) and

Andrew, Peter's brother;

James and John, Philip and Bartholomew;

15 Matthew, Thomas, James son of Alphaeus, and Simon (called the Zealot[d]),

16 Judas son of James and Judas Iscariot. This Judas was the one who gave Jesus to his enemies.

Jesus Teaches and Heals

17 Jesus and the apostles[d] came down from the mountain. Jesus stood on level ground where there was a large group of his followers. Also, there were many people from all around Judea, Jerusalem, and the seacoast cities of Tyre and Sidon. 18 They all came to hear Jesus teach and to be healed of their sicknesses. He healed those who were troubled by evil spirits. 19 All the people were trying to touch Jesus, because power was coming from him and healing them all!

20 Jesus looked at his followers and said,

"Poor people, you are happy, because God's kingdom belongs to you. 21 You people who are now hungry are happy, because you will be satisfied. You people who are now crying are happy, because you will laugh with joy.
22 "You are happy when people hate you and are cruel to you. You are happy when they say that you are evil because you belong to the Son of Man.[d]
23 At that time be full of joy, because you have a great reward in heaven. Their fathers were cruel to the prophets[d] in the same way these people are cruel to you.
24 "But how terrible it will be for you who are rich, because you have had your easy life.
25 How terrible it will be for you who are full now, because you will be hungry. How terrible it will be for you who are laughing now, because you will be sad and cry.
26 "How terrible when all people say only good things about you. Their fathers always said good things about the false prophets.

Love Your Enemies

27 "I say to you who are listening to me, love your enemies. Do good to those who hate you.
28 Ask God to bless those who say bad things to you. Pray for those who are cruel to you.
29 If anyone slaps you on one cheek, let him slap the other cheek too. If someone takes your coat, do not stop him from taking your shirt. 30 Give to everyone who asks you. When a person takes something that is yours, don't ask for it back.
31 Do for other people what you want them to do for you.
32 If you love only those who love you, should you get some special praise for doing that? No! Even sinners love the people who love them!

Luke 6:33-47

33 "If you do good only to those who do good to you, should you get some special praise for doing that? No! Even sinners do that! 34 If you lend things to people, always hoping to get something back, should you get some special praise for that? No! Even sinners lend to other sinners so that they can get back the same amount! 35 So love your enemies. Do good to them, and lend to them without hoping to get anything back. If you do these things, you will have a great reward. You will be sons of the Most High God. Yes, because God is kind even to people who are ungrateful and full of sin. 36 Show mercy just as your father shows mercy.

Look at Yourselves

37 "Don't judge other people, and you will not be judged. Don't accuse others of being guilty, and you will not be accused of being guilty. Forgive other people, and you will be forgiven.

38 Give, and you will receive. You will be given much. It will be poured into your hands—more than you can hold. You will be given so much that it will spill into your lap. The way you give to others is the way God will give to you."

39 Jesus told them this story:

"Can a blind man lead another blind man? No! Both of them will fall into a ditch. 40 A student is not better than his teacher. But when the student has fully learned all that he has been taught, then he will be like his teacher.
41 "Why do you notice the little piece of dust that is in your brother's eye, but you don't see the big piece of wood that is in your own eye? 42 You say to your brother, 'Brother, let me take that little piece of dust out of your eye.' Why do you say this? You cannot see that big piece of wood in your own eye! You are a hypocrite![d] First, take the

piece of wood out of your own eye. Then you will see clearly to take the dust out of your brother's eye.

Two Kinds of Fruit

43 "A good tree does not produce bad fruit. Also, a bad tree does not produce good fruit. 44 Each tree is known by its fruit. People don't gather figs from thornbushes. And they don't get grapes from bushes. 45 A good person has good things saved up in his heart. And so he brings good things out of his heart. But an evil person has evil things saved up in his heart. So he brings out bad things. A person speaks the things that are in his heart.

Two Kinds of People

46 "Why do you call me, 'Lord, Lord,' but do not do what I say? 47 Everyone who comes to me and listens to my words and obeys

48 is like a man building a house. He digs deep and lays his foundation on rock. The floods come, and the water tries to wash the house away. But the flood cannot move the house, because the house was built well.

49 But the one who hears my words and does not obey is like a man who builds his house on the ground without a foundation. When the floods come, the house quickly falls down. And that house is completely destroyed."

Chapter

7

Jesus Heals a Soldier's Servant

1 When Jesus finished saying all these things to the people, he went to Capernaum.

2 In Capernaum there was an army officer. He had a servant who was so sick he was nearly dead. The officer loved the servant very much. 3 When the officer heard about Jesus, he sent some Jewish elders to him. The officer wanted the leaders to ask Jesus to come and heal his servant.
4 The men went to Jesus and begged him saying,

"This officer is worthy of your help. 5 He loves our people, and he built us a synagogue."[d]

31

6 So Jesus went with the men. He was getting near the officer's house when the officer sent friends to say,

"Lord, you don't need to come into my house. I am not good enough for you to be under my roof. 7 That is why I did not come to you myself. You only need to say the word, and my servant will be healed. 8 I, too, am a man under the authority of other men. And I have soldiers under my command. I tell one soldier, 'Go,' and he goes. And I tell another soldier, 'Come,' and he comes. And I say to my servant, 'Do this,' and my servant obeys me."

9 When Jesus heard this, he was amazed. He turned to the crowd following him and said,

"I tell you, this is the greatest faith I have seen anywhere, even in Israel."

10 The men who had been sent to Jesus went back to the house. There they found that the servant was healed.

Jesus Brings a Man Back to Life

11 The next day Jesus went to a town called Nain. His followers and a large crowd were traveling with him. 12 When he came near the town gate, he saw a funeral. A mother, who was a widow, had lost her only son. A large crowd from the town was with the mother while her son was being carried out.

13 When the Lord saw her, he felt very sorry for her. Jesus said to her,

"Don't cry."

14 He went up to the coffin and touched it. The men who were carrying it stopped. Jesus said,

"Young man, I tell you, get up!"

15 And the son sat up and began to talk.

Then Jesus gave him back to his mother.

16 All the people were amazed. They began praising God. They said,

"A great prophet[d] has come to us!

God is taking care of his people."

17 This news about Jesus spread through all Judea and into all the places around there.

John Asks a Question

18 John's followers told him about all these things. He called for two of his followers.

19 He sent them to the Lord to ask,

"Are you the One who is coming, or should we wait for another?"

20 So the men came to Jesus. They said,

"John the Baptist[d] sent us to you with this question: 'Are you the One who is coming, or should we wait for another?' "

21 At that time, Jesus healed many people of their sicknesses, diseases, and evil spirits. He healed many blind people so that they could see again. 22 Then Jesus said to John's followers,

"Go tell John the things that you saw and heard here. The blind can see. The crippled can walk. People with a harmful skin disease are healed. The deaf can hear, and the dead are given life.

And the Good News[d] is told to the poor. 23 The person who does not lose faith is blessed!"

24 When John's followers left, Jesus began to tell the people about John:

"What did you go out into the desert to see? A reed[n] blown by the wind? 25 What did you go out to see? A man dressed in fine clothes? No. People who have fine clothes live in kings' palaces.

7:24 reed It means that John was not weak like grass blown by the wind.

26 "But what did you go out to see? A prophet?[d] Yes, and I tell you, John is more than a prophet. 27 This was written about John:

'I will send my messenger ahead of you. He will prepare the way for you.'

Malachi 3:1

28 I tell you, John is greater than any other man ever born. But even the least important person in the kingdom of God is greater than John."

29 (When the people heard this, they all agreed that God's teaching was good. Even the tax collectors agreed. These were people who were already baptized by John. 30 But the Pharisees[d] and teachers of the law refused to accept God's plan for themselves; they did not let John baptize them.) 31 Then Jesus said,

"What shall I say about the people of this time? What are they like? 32 They are like children sitting in the marketplace. One group of children calls to the other group and says, 'We played music for you, but you did not dance. We sang a sad song, but you did not cry.' 33 John the Baptist came and did not eat like other people or drink wine. And you say, 'He has a demon[d] in him.' 34 The Son of Man[d] came eating like other people and drinking wine. And you say, 'Look at him! He eats too much and drinks too much wine! He is a friend of the tax collectors and "sinners"!' 35 But wisdom is shown to be right by the things it does."

Simon the Pharisee

36 One of the Pharisees[d] asked Jesus to eat with him. Jesus went into the Pharisee's house and sat at the table. 37 A sinful woman in the town learned that Jesus was eating at the Pharisee's house. So she brought an alabaster[d] jar of perfume.

34

38 She stood at Jesus' feet, crying, and began to wash his feet with her tears. She dried his feet with her hair, kissed them many times and rubbed them with the perfume.

39 The Pharisee who asked Jesus to come to his house saw this. He thought to himself,

"If Jesus were a prophet,[d] he would know that the woman who is touching him is a sinner!"

40 Jesus said to the Pharisee,

"Simon, I have something to say to you."

Simon said,

"Teacher, tell me."

41 Jesus said, "There were two men. Both men owed money to the same banker. One man owed the banker 500 silver coins.[n] The other man owed the banker 50 silver coins. 42 The men had no money; so they could not pay what they owed. But the banker told the men that they did not have to pay him. Which one of the two men will love the banker more?"

43 Simon, the Pharisee, answered,

"I think it would be the one who owed him the most money."

Jesus said to Simon,

"You are right."

44 Then Jesus turned toward the woman and said to Simon,

"Do you see this woman? When I came into your house, you gave me no water for my feet. But she washed my feet with her tears and dried my feet with her hair. 45 You did not kiss me, but she has been kissing my feet since I came in!

7:41 silver coins A Roman denarius. One coin was the average pay for one day's work.

46 "You did not rub my head with oil, but she rubbed my feet with perfume. 47 I tell you that her many sins are forgiven. This is clear because she showed great love. But the person who has only a little to be forgiven will feel only a little love."

48 Then Jesus said to her,

"Your sins are forgiven."

49 The people sitting at the table began to think to themselves,

"Who is this man? How can he forgive sins?"

50 Jesus said to the woman,

"Because you believed, you are saved from your sins. Go in peace."

Chapter
8

The Group with Jesus

1 The next day, while Jesus was traveling through some cities and small towns, he preached and told the Good News[d] about God's kingdom. The 12 apostles[d] were with him.

2 There were also some women with him who had been healed of sicknesses and evil spirits. One of the women was Mary, called Magdalene, from whom seven demons[d] had gone out. 3 Also among the women were Joanna, the wife of Chuza (Herod's helper), Susanna, and many other women. These women used their own money to help Jesus and his apostles.

A Story About Planting Seed

4 A great crowd gathered. People were coming to Jesus from every town. He told them this story:

5 "A farmer went out to plant his seed. While he was planting, some seed fell beside the road.

People walked on the seed, and the birds ate all this seed.

6 Some seed fell on rock.

It began to grow but then died because it had no water.

7 Some seed fell among thorny weeds. This seed grew, but later the weeds choked the good plants.

8 And some seed fell on good ground.

This seed grew and made 100 times more grain."

Jesus finished the story. Then he called out,

"Let those with ears use them and listen!"

9 Jesus' followers asked him,

"What does this story mean?"

10 Jesus said,

"You have been chosen to know the secret truths of the kingdom of God. But I use stories to speak to other people. I do this so that:

'They will look, but they may not see. They will listen, but they may not understand.'   *Isaiah 6:9*

11 "This is what the story means: The seed is God's teaching.

12 What is the seed that fell beside the road? It is like the people who hear God's teaching, but then the devil comes and takes it away from their hearts. So they cannot believe the teaching and be saved.

13 What is the seed that fell on rock? It is like those who hear God's teaching and accept it gladly. But they don't have deep roots. They believe for a while, but then trouble comes. They stop believing and turn away from God.

14 What is the seed that fell among the thorny weeds? It is like those who hear God's teaching, but they let the worries, riches, and pleasures of this life keep them from growing. So they never produce good fruit.

15 And what is the seed that fell on the good ground? That is like those who hear God's teaching with a good, honest heart. They obey God's teaching and patiently produce good fruit.

Use What You Have

16 "No one lights a lamp and then covers it with a bowl

or hides it under a bed.

Instead, he puts the lamp on a lampstand so that those who come in will have enough light to see.

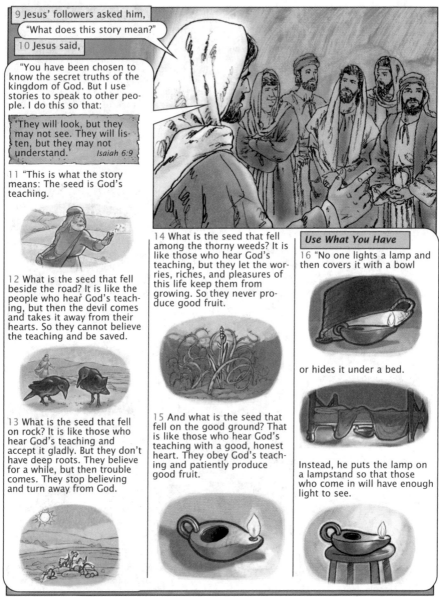

17 "Everything that is hidden will become clear. Every secret thing will be made known. 18 So be careful how you listen. The person who has something will be given more. But to the person who has nothing, this will happen: Even what he thinks he has will be taken away from him."

Jesus' True Family

19 Jesus' mother and brothers came to see him. There was such a crowd that they could not get to him. 20 Someone said to Jesus,

"Your mother and your brothers are standing outside. They want to see you."

21 Jesus answered them,

"My mother and my brothers are those who listen to God's teaching and obey it!"

Jesus Stops a Storm

22 One day Jesus and his followers got into a boat. He said to them,

"Come with me across the lake."

And so they started across.

23 While they were sailing, Jesus fell asleep.

A big storm blew up on the lake. The boat began to fill with water, and they were in danger.

39

Luke 8:24-25

24 The followers went to Jesus and woke him. They said,

"Master! Master! We will drown!"

Jesus got up

and gave a command to the wind and the waves.

The wind stopped, and the lake became calm.

25 Jesus said to his followers,

"Where is your faith?"

The followers were afraid and amazed. They said to each other,

"What kind of man is this? He commands the wind and the water, and they obey him!"

A Man with Demons Inside Him

26 Jesus and his followers sailed across the lake from Galilee to the area where the Gerasene[n] people live.

27 When Jesus got out of the boat, a man from the town came to Jesus. This man had demons[d] inside him. For a long time he had worn no clothes. He lived in the burial caves, not in a house. 28 When he saw Jesus, he cried out and fell down before him. The man said with a loud voice,

"What do you want with me, Jesus, Son of the Most High God?"

"Please don't punish me!"

29 He said this because Jesus had commanded the evil spirit to come out of him. Many times it had taken hold of him. He had been kept under guard and chained hand and foot. But he had broken his chains and had been driven by the demon out into the desert.

30 Jesus asked him,

What is your name?

The man answered,

"Legion."[n]

(He said his name was "Legion" because many demons were in him.) 31 The demons begged Jesus not to send them into eternal darkness.[n]

32 On the hill there was a large herd of pigs eating. The demons begged Jesus to allow them to go into the pigs. So Jesus allowed them to do this.

33 Then the demons came out of the man and went into the pigs. The herd of pigs ran down the hill and into the lake. All the pigs drowned.

8:26 **Gerasene** From Gerasa, an area southeast of Lake Galilee. The exact location is uncertain and some Greek copies read "Gadarene"; others read "Gergesene."
8:30 **"Legion"** Means very many. A legion was about 5,000 men in the Roman army.
8:31 **eternal darkness** Literally, "the abyss," something like a pit or a hole that has no end.

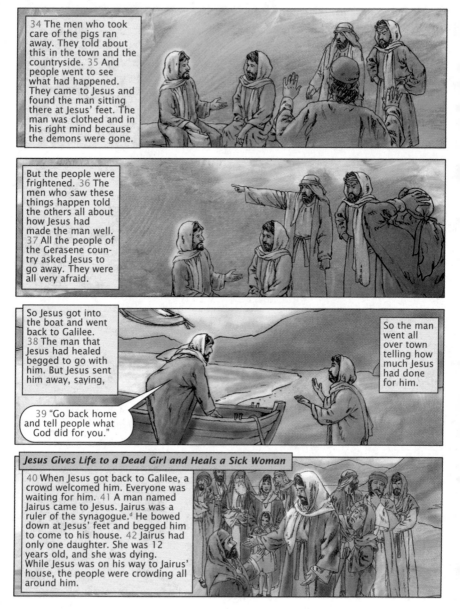

34 The men who took care of the pigs ran away. They told about this in the town and the countryside. 35 And people went to see what had happened. They came to Jesus and found the man sitting there at Jesus' feet. The man was clothed and in his right mind because the demons were gone.

But the people were frightened. 36 The men who saw these things happen told the others all about how Jesus had made the man well. 37 All the people of the Gerasene country asked Jesus to go away. They were all very afraid.

So Jesus got into the boat and went back to Galilee. 38 The man that Jesus had healed begged to go with him. But Jesus sent him away, saying,

39 "Go back home and tell people what God did for you."

So the man went all over town telling how much Jesus had done for him.

Jesus Gives Life to a Dead Girl and Heals a Sick Woman

40 When Jesus got back to Galilee, a crowd welcomed him. Everyone was waiting for him. 41 A man named Jairus came to Jesus. Jairus was a ruler of the synagogue.[d] He bowed down at Jesus' feet and begged him to come to his house. 42 Jairus had only one daughter. She was 12 years old, and she was dying. While Jesus was on his way to Jairus' house, the people were crowding all around him.

43 A woman was there who had been bleeding for 12 years. She had spent all her money on doctors, but no doctor was able to heal her. 44 The woman came up behind Jesus

and touched the edge of his coat.

At that moment, her bleeding stopped.

45 Then Jesus said,

"Who touched me?"

All the people said they had not touched Jesus. Peter said,

"Master, the people are all around you and are pushing against you."

46 But Jesus said,

"Someone did touch me! I felt power go out from me."

47 When the woman saw that she could not hide, she came forward, shaking. She bowed down before Jesus. While all the people listened, she told why she had touched him. Then, she said, she was healed immediately. 48 Jesus said to her,

"Dear woman, you are healed because you believed. Go in peace."

49 While Jesus was still speaking, someone came from the house of the synagogue ruler and said to the ruler,

"Your daughter has died! Don't bother the teacher now."

50 When Jesus heard this, he said to Jairus,

"Don't be afraid. Just believe, and your daughter will be well."

43

55 Her spirit came back into her, and she stood up immediately. Jesus said,

"Give her something to eat."

56 The girl's parents were amazed. Jesus told them not to tell anyone about what happened.

Chapter 9

Jesus Sends Out the Apostles

1 Jesus called the 12 apostles[d] together. He gave them power to heal sicknesses and power over all demons.[d] 2 Jesus sent the apostles out to tell about God's kingdom and to heal the sick. 3 He said to them,

"When you travel, don't take a walking stick. Also, don't carry a bag, or food, or money. Take for your trip only the clothes you are wearing. 4 When you go into a house, stay there until it is time to leave. 5 If the people in the town will not welcome you, go outside the town and shake the dust off of your feet.[n] This will be a warning to them."

6 So the apostles went out. They traveled through all the towns. They told the Good News[d] and healed people everywhere.

9:5 shake . . . feet A warning. It showed that they were finished talking to these people.

Luke 9:7-14

Herod Is Confused About Jesus

7 Herod, the governor, heard about all these things that were happening. He was confused because some people said, "John the Baptist[d] is risen from death." 8 Others said, "Elijah has come to us." And still others said, "One of the prophets[d] from long ago has risen from death."

9 Herod said,

"I cut off John's head. So who is this man I hear these things about?"

And Herod kept trying to see Jesus.

More than 5,000 People Fed

10 When the apostles[d] returned, they told Jesus all the things they had done on their trip. Then Jesus took them away to a town called Bethsaida. There, Jesus and his apostles could be alone together.

11 But the people learned where Jesus went and followed him. Jesus welcomed them and talked with them about God's kingdom. He healed those who needed to be healed.

12 Late in the afternoon, the 12 apostles came to Jesus and said,

"No one lives in this place. Send the people away. They need to find food and places to sleep in the towns and countryside around here."

13 But Jesus said to them,

"You give them something to eat."

They said,

"We have only five loaves of bread and two fish. Do you want us to go buy food for all these people?"

14 (There were about 5,000 men there.) Jesus said to his followers,

"Tell the people to sit in groups of about 50 people."

15 So the followers did this, and all the people sat down.
16 Then Jesus took the five loaves of bread and two fish. He looked up to heaven and thanked God for the food.

Then Jesus divided the food and gave it to the followers to give to the people. 17 All the people ate and were satisfied. And there was much food left. Twelve baskets were filled with pieces of food that were not eaten.

Jesus Is the Christ

18 One time when Jesus was praying alone, his followers came together there. Jesus asked them,

"Who do the people say I am?"

19 They answered,

"Some say you are John the Baptist.d Others say you are Elijah.n And others say you are one of the prophetsd from long ago who has come back to life."

9:19 Elijah A man who spoke for God. He lived hundreds of years before Christ.

47

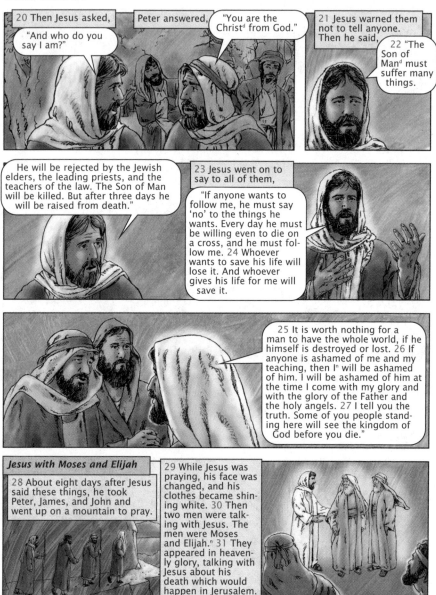

20 Then Jesus asked, "And who do you say I am?"

Peter answered, "You are the Christ[d] from God."

21 Jesus warned them not to tell anyone. Then he said, 22 "The Son of Man[d] must suffer many things.

He will be rejected by the Jewish elders, the leading priests, and the teachers of the law. The Son of Man will be killed. But after three days he will be raised from death."

23 Jesus went on to say to all of them, "If anyone wants to follow me, he must say 'no' to the things he wants. Every day he must be willing even to die on a cross, and he must follow me. 24 Whoever wants to save his life will lose it. And whoever gives his life for me will save it.

25 It is worth nothing for a man to have the whole world, if he himself is destroyed or lost. 26 If anyone is ashamed of me and my teaching, then I[n] will be ashamed of him. I will be ashamed of him at the time I come with my glory and with the glory of the Father and the holy angels. 27 I tell you the truth. Some of you people standing here will see the kingdom of God before you die."

Jesus with Moses and Elijah

28 About eight days after Jesus said these things, he took Peter, James, and John and went up on a mountain to pray.

29 While Jesus was praying, his face was changed, and his clothes became shining white. 30 Then two men were talking with Jesus. The men were Moses and Elijah.[n] 31 They appeared in heavenly glory, talking with Jesus about his death which would happen in Jerusalem.

9:26 I Literally, "the Son of Man."
9:30 **Moses and Elijah** Two of the most important Jewish leaders in the past.

32 Peter and the others were asleep. But they woke up and saw the glory of Jesus. They also saw the two men who were standing with him.

33 When Moses and Elijah were about to leave, Peter said,

"Master, it is good that we are here. We will put three tents here—

one for you, one for Moses, and one for Elijah."

(Peter did not know what he was saying.)

34 While Peter was saying these things, a cloud came down all around them. Peter, James, and John became afraid when the cloud covered them. 35 A voice came from the cloud. The voice said,

"This is my Son. He is the One I have chosen. Obey him."

36 When the voice finished speaking, only Jesus was there. Peter, James, and John said nothing. At that time they told no one about what they had seen.

Jesus Heals a Sick Boy

37 The next day, Jesus, Peter, James, and John came down from the mountain. A large crowd met Jesus. 38 A man in the crowd shouted to Jesus,

"Teacher, please come and look at my son. He is the only child I have. 39 An evil spirit comes into my son, and then he shouts. He loses control of himself, and he foams at the mouth. The evil spirit keeps on hurting him and almost never leaves him. 40 I begged your followers to make the evil spirit leave my son, but they could not do it."

41 Jesus answered,

"You people who live now have no faith. Your lives are all wrong. How long must I be with you and be patient with you?"

Then Jesus said to the man,

"Bring your son here."

42 While the boy was coming, the demon[d] threw him on the ground. The boy lost control of himself.

But Jesus gave a strong command to the evil spirit. Then the boy was healed,

and Jesus gave him back to his father.

43 All the people were amazed at the great power of God.

Jesus Talks About His Death

The people were all wondering about the things Jesus did. But he said to his followers,

44 "Don't forget the things I tell you now: The Son of Man[d] will be handed over into the control of men."

45 But the followers did not understand what Jesus meant. The meaning was hidden from them so that they could not understand it. But they were afraid to ask Jesus about what he said.

The Most Important Person

46 Jesus' followers began to have an argument about which one of them was the greatest.

47 Jesus knew what they were thinking. So he took a little child and stood the child beside him.

48 Then Jesus said,

"If anyone accepts a little child like this in my name, then he accepts me. And when he accepts me, he accepts the One who sent me. He who is least among you all—he is the greatest."

Anyone Not Against Us Is for Us

49 John answered,

"Master, we saw someone using your name to force demons[d] out of people. We told him to stop because he does not belong to our group."

50 Jesus said to him,

"Don't stop him. If a person is not against you, then he is for you."

A Samaritan Town

51 The time was coming near when Jesus would leave and be taken to heaven. He was determined to go to Jerusalem 52 and sent some men ahead of him.

The men went into a town in Samaria to make everything ready for Jesus. 53 But the people there would not welcome him because he was going toward Jerusalem.

54 James and John, the followers of Jesus, saw this. They said,

"Lord, do you want us to call fire down from heaven and destroy those people?"[n]

55 But Jesus turned and scolded them.[n] And Jesus said,

"You don't know what kind of spirit you belong to. 56 The Son of Man did not come to destroy the souls of men but to save them."[n]

Then they went to another town.

Following Jesus

57 They were all going along the road. Someone said to Jesus,

"I will follow you any place you go."

58 Jesus answered,

"The foxes have holes to live in. The birds have nests to live in. But the Son of Man[d] has no place to rest his head."

59 Jesus said to another man,

"Follow me!"

9:54 people Some Greek copies add: ". . . as Elijah did."
9:55-56 And . . . them. Some Greek copies do not contain the bracketed text.

Luke 9:60–10:16

But the man said,

"Lord, first let me go and bury my father."

60 But Jesus said to him,

"Let the people who are dead bury their own dead! You must go and tell about the kingdom of God."

61 Another man said,

"I will follow you, Lord, but first let me go and say good-bye to my family."

62 Jesus said,

"Anyone who begins to plow a field but keeps looking back is of no use in the kingdom of God."

Chapter 10

Jesus Sends the 72 Men

1 After this, the Lord chose 72[n] others. He sent them out in pairs. He sent them ahead of him into every town and place where he planned to go.

2 He said to them, "There are a great many people to harvest. But there are only a few workers to harvest them. God owns the harvest. Pray to God that he will send more workers to help gather his harvest. 3 You can go now. But listen! I am sending you, and you will be like sheep among wolves. 4 Don't carry a purse, a bag, or sandals. Don't stop to talk with people on the road. 5 Before you go into a house, say, 'Peace be with this house.' 6 If a peaceful man lives there, your blessing of peace will stay with him. If the man is not peaceful, then your blessing of peace will come back to you. 7 Stay in the same house. Eat and drink what the people there give you. A worker should be given his pay. Don't move from house to house. 8 If you go into a town and the people welcome you, eat what they give you. 9 Heal the sick who live there. Tell them, 'The kingdom of God is soon coming to you!' 10 But if you go into a town, and the people don't welcome you, then go out into the streets of that town. Say to them, 11 'Even the dirt from your town that sticks to our feet we wipe off against you.[n] But remember that the kingdom of God is coming soon.' 12 I tell you, on the Judgment Day it will be worse for the people of that town than for the people of Sodom.[n]

Jesus Warns Unbelievers

13 "How terrible for you, Korazin! How terrible for you, Bethsaida! I did many miracles[d] in you. If those same miracles had happened in Tyre and Sidon,[n] those people would have changed their lives and stopped sinning long ago. They would have worn rough cloth and put ashes on themselves to show that they had changed. 14 But on the Judgment Day it will be worse for you than for Tyre and Sidon. 15 And you, Capernaum,[n] will you be lifted up to heaven? No! You will be thrown down to the depths! 16 "He who listens to you is really listening to me. He who refuses to accept you is really refusing to accept me. And he who refuses to accept me is refusing to accept the One who sent me."

10:1 **72** Some Greek copies read "70." **10:11 dirt . . . you** A warning. It showed that they were finished talking to these people. **10:12 Sodom** City that God destroyed because the people were so evil. **10:13 Tyre and Sidon** Towns where wicked people lived. **10:13-15 Korazin . . . Bethsaida . . . Capernaum** Towns by Lake Galilee where Jesus preached to the people.

Satan Falls

17 When the 72ⁿ men came back from their trip, they were very happy.

They said, "Lord, even the demonsᵈ obeyed us when we used your name!"

18 Jesus said to the men,

"I saw Satan falling like lightning from the sky. 19 Listen! I gave you power to walk on snakes and scorpions. I gave you more power than the Enemy has. Nothing will hurt you. 20 You should be happy, but not because the spirits obey you. You should be happy because your names are written in heaven."

Jesus Prays to the Father

21 Then the Holy Spiritᵈ made Jesus rejoice. He said,

"I thank you, Father, Lord of heaven and earth, because you have hidden these things from the people who are wise and smart.

But you have shown them to those who are like little children. Yes, Father, you did this because this is what you really wanted.

22 "My Father has given me all things. No one knows the Son—only the Father knows. And only the Son knows the Father. The only people who will know about the Father are those whom the Son chooses to tell."

23 Then Jesus turned to his followers and said privately,

"You are blessed to see what you now see! 24 I tell you, many prophetsᵈ and kings wanted to see what you now see. But they did not see these things. And many prophets and kings wanted to hear what you now hear. But they did not hear these things."

10:17 72 Some Greek copies read "70."

53

Luke 10:25-34

The Good Samaritan

25 Then a teacher of the law stood up. He was trying to test Jesus. He said,

"Teacher, what must I do to get life forever?"

26 Jesus said to him,

"What is written in the law? What do you read there?"

27 The man answered,

"Love the Lord your God. Love him with all your heart, all your soul, all your strength, and all your mind."[n] Also,

"You must love your neighbor as you love yourself."[n]

28 Jesus said to him,

"Your answer is right. Do this and you will have life forever."

29 But the man wanted to show that the way he was living was right. So he said to Jesus,

"And who is my neighbor?"

30 To answer this question, Jesus said,

"A man was going down the road from Jerusalem to Jericho. Some robbers attacked him. They tore off his clothes and beat him. Then they left him lying there, almost dead.

31 It happened that a Jewish priest was going down that road. When the priest saw the man, he walked by on the other side of the road.

32 Next, a Levite[n] came there. He went over and looked at the man. Then he walked by on the other side of the road.

33 Then a Samaritan[n] traveling down the road came to where the hurt man was lying. He saw the man and felt very sorry for him.

34 The Samaritan went to him and poured olive oil and wine[n] on his wounds and bandaged them. He put the hurt man on his own donkey and took him to an inn. At the inn, the Samaritan took care of him.

10:27 "Love . . . mind." Quotation from Deuteronomy 6:5. **10:27 "You . . . yourself."** Quotation from Leviticus 19:18. **10:32 Levite** Levites were men from the tribe of Levi who helped the Jewish priests with their work in the Temple. Read 1 Chronicles 23:24-32. **10:33 Samaritan** Samaritans were people from Samaria. These people were part Jewish, but the Jews did not accept them as true Jews. Samaritans and Jews hated each other. **10:34 olive oil and wine** Oil and wine were used like medicine to soften and clean wounds.

35 "The next day, the Samaritan brought out two silver coins[n] and gave them to the innkeeper. The Samaritan said, 'Take care of this man. If you spend more money on him, I will pay it back to you when I come again.'"

36 Then Jesus said,

"Which one of these three men do you think was a neighbor to the man who was attacked by the robbers?"

37 The teacher of the law answered,

"The one who helped him."

Jesus said to him,

"Then go and do the same thing he did!"

Mary and Martha

38 While Jesus and his followers were traveling, Jesus went into a town.

A woman named Martha let Jesus stay at her house. 39 Martha had a sister named Mary. Mary was sitting at Jesus' feet and listening to him teach. 40 Martha became angry because she had so much work to do.

10:35 silver coins A Roman denarius. One coin was the average pay for one day's work.

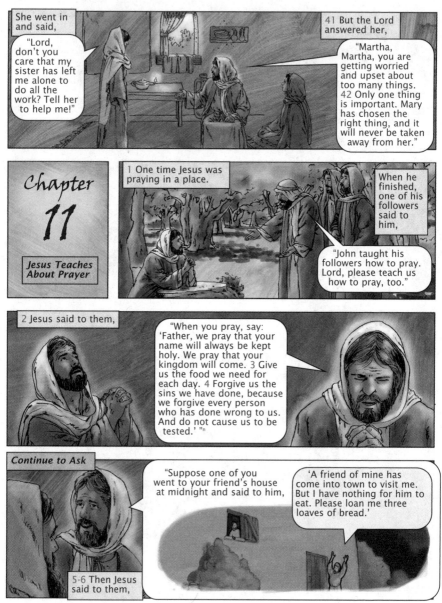

11:2-4 'Father . . . tested.' Some Greek copies include phrases from Matthew's version of this prayer (Matthew 6:9-13).

7 "Your friend inside the house answers,

'Don't bother me! The door is already locked. My children and I are in bed. I cannot get up and give you the bread now.'

8 I tell you, maybe friendship is not enough to make him get up to give you the bread. But he will surely get up to give you what you need if you continue to ask.

9 So I tell you, continue to ask, and God will give to you. Continue to search, and you will find. Continue to knock, and the door will open for you. 10 Yes, if a person continues asking, he will receive. If he continues searching, he will find. And if he continues knocking, the door will open for him. 11 What would you fathers do if your son asks you for[n] a fish? Would any of you give him a snake? 12 Or, if your son asks for an egg,

would you give him a scorpion?

13 Even though you are bad, you know how to give good things to your children. So surely your heavenly Father knows how to give the Holy Spirit[d] to those who ask him."

Jesus' Power Is from God

14 One time Jesus was sending a demon[d] out of a man who could not talk. When the demon came out, the man was able to speak. The people were amazed. 15 But some of them said,

"Jesus uses the power of Beelzebul[d] to force demons out of people. Beelzebul is the ruler of demons."

16 Other people wanted to test Jesus. They asked him to give them a sign from heaven.

17 But Jesus knew what they were thinking. So he said to them,

"Every kingdom that is divided and fights against itself will be destroyed. And a family that fights against itself will break apart. 18 So if Satan is fighting against himself, then how will his kingdom last? You say that I use the power of Beelzebul to force out demons.

19 But if I use the power of Beelzebul to force out demons, then by what power do your people force out demons? So your own people prove that you are wrong. 20 But if I use the power of God to force out demons, the kingdom of God has come to you!

11:11 for Some Greek copies include the phrase "for bread? Would any of you give him a stone? Or if he asks you for . . ." and continue to verse 12.

21 "When a strong man with many weapons guards his own house, then the things in his house are safe. 22 But suppose a stronger man comes and defeats him. The stronger man will take away the weapons that the first man trusted to keep his house safe. Then the stronger man will do what he wants with the first man's things.

23 "If anyone is not with me, he is against me. He who does not work with me is working against me.

The Empty Man

24 "When an evil spirit comes out of a person, it travels through dry places, looking for a place to rest. But that spirit finds no place to rest. So it says, 'I will go back to the home I left.' 25 When the spirit comes back to that person, it finds that home swept clean and made neat. 26 Then the evil spirit goes out and brings seven other spirits more evil than itself. Then all the evil spirits go into that person and live there. And he has even more trouble than he had before."

People Who Are Truly Blessed

27 When Jesus was saying these things, a woman in the crowd spoke out. She said to Jesus,

"Your mother is blessed because she gave birth to you and nursed you."

28 But Jesus said,

"Those who hear the teaching of God and obey it— they are the ones who are truly blessed."

Give Us Proof!

29 The crowd grew larger. Jesus said,

"The people who live today are evil. They ask for a miracle[d] as a sign from God. But they will have no sign—only the sign of Jonah.[n] 30 Jonah was a sign for those people who lived in Nineveh. In the same way the Son of Man[d] will be a sign for the people of this time.

31 On the Judgment Day the Queen of the South[n] will stand up with the men who live now. She will show that they are guilty because she came from far away to listen to Solomon's wise teaching. And I tell you that someone greater than Solomon is here!

11:29 sign of Jonah Jonah's three days in the big fish are like Jesus' three days in the tomb. **11:31 Queen of the South** The Queen of Sheba. She traveled 1,000 miles to learn God's wisdom from Solomon. Read 1 Kings 10:1-3.

Instead, he puts the light on a lampstand so that the people who come in can see.

34 Your eye is a light for the body. If your eyes are good, then your whole body will be full of light. But if your eyes are evil, then your whole body will be full of darkness. 35 So be careful! Don't let the light in you become darkness. 36 If your whole body is full of light, and none of it is dark, then you will shine bright, as when a lamp shines on you."

32 "On the Judgment Day the men of Nineveh will stand up with the people who live now. And they will show that you are guilty, because when Jonah preached to those people, they changed their hearts and lives. And I tell you that someone greater than Jonah is here!

Be a Light for the World

33 "No one takes a light and puts it under a bowl or hides it.

Jesus Accuses the Pharisees

37 After Jesus had finished speaking, a Pharisee[d] asked Jesus to eat with him. So Jesus went in and sat at the table. 38 But the Pharisee was surprised when he saw that Jesus did not wash his hands[n] before the meal. 39 The Lord said to him,

"You Pharisees clean the outside of the cup and the dish. But inside you are full of greed and evil. 40 You are foolish. The same One who made what is outside also made what is inside. 41 So give what is in your cups and dishes to the poor. Then you will be fully clean.

42 But how terrible for you Pharisees! You give God one-tenth of even your mint, your rue, and every other plant in your garden. But you forget to be fair to other people and to love God. These are the things you should do. And you should also continue to do those other things—like giving one-tenth. 43 How terrible for you Pharisees, because you love to get the most important seats in the synagogues.[d] And you love people to show respect to you in the marketplaces.

44 How terrible for you, because you are like hidden graves. People walk on them without knowing it."

11:38 wash his hands This was a Jewish religious custom that the Pharisees thought was very important.

Luke 11:45-54

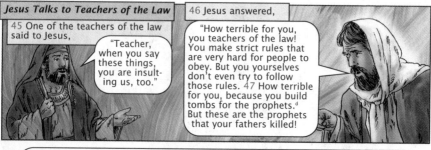

Jesus Talks to Teachers of the Law

45 One of the teachers of the law said to Jesus,

"Teacher, when you say these things, you are insulting us, too."

46 Jesus answered,

"How terrible for you, you teachers of the law! You make strict rules that are very hard for people to obey. But you yourselves don't even try to follow those rules. 47 How terrible for you, because you build tombs for the prophets.[d] But these are the prophets that your fathers killed!

48 And now you show that you approve of what your fathers did. They killed the prophets, and you build tombs for the prophets! 49 This is why in his wisdom God said, 'I will send prophets and apostles[d] to them. Some of my prophets and apostles will be killed, and others will be treated cruelly.' 50 So you who live now will be punished for the deaths of all the prophets who were killed since the beginning of the world. 51 You will be punished for the killing of Abel and for the killing of Zechariah.[n] Zechariah was killed between the altar and the Temple.[d] Yes, I tell you that you people who live now will be punished for them all.

52 "How terrible for you, you teachers of the law. You have hidden the key to learning about God. You yourselves would not learn, and you stopped others from learning, too."

53 When Jesus was leaving, the teachers of the law and the Pharisees[d] began to give him trouble, asking him questions about many things. 54 They were trying to catch Jesus saying something wrong.

Chapter
12

Don't Be Like the Pharisees

11:51 Abel . . . Zechariah In the Hebrew Old Testament, the first and last men to be murdered.

1 Many thousands of people had gathered. There were so many people that they were stepping on each other. Before Jesus spoke to them, he said to his followers,

"Be careful of the yeast of the Pharisees.[d] They are hypocrites.[d] 2 Everything that is hidden will be shown. Everything that is secret will be made known. 3 The things you say in the dark will be told in the light. The things you have whispered in an inner room will be shouted from the top of the house."

Fear Only God

4 Then Jesus said to the people,

"I tell you, my friends, don't be afraid of people.

People can kill the body, but after that they can do nothing more to hurt you. 5 I will show you the One to fear. You should fear him who has the power to kill you and also to throw you into hell. Yes, he is the One you should fear. 6 "When five sparrows are sold, they cost only two pennies. But God does not forget any of them. 7 Yes, God even knows how many hairs you have on your head. Don't be afraid. You are worth much more than many sparrows.

Don't Be Ashamed of Jesus

8 "I tell you, if anyone stands before others and says that he believes in me, then I will say that he belongs to me. I will say

this before the angels of God. 9 But if anyone stands before others and says he does not believe in me, then I will say that he does not belong to me. I will say this before the angels of God.
10 "If a person says something against the Son of Man,[d] he can be forgiven. But a person who says bad things against the Holy Spirit[d] will not be forgiven. 11 "When men bring you into the synagogues[d] before the leaders and other important men, don't worry about how to defend yourself or what to say. 12 At that time the Holy Spirit will teach you what you must say."

Jesus Warns Against Selfishness

13 One of the men in the crowd said to Jesus,

"Teacher, tell my brother to divide with me the property our father left us."

14 But Jesus said to him,

"Who said that I should be your judge or decide how to divide the property between you two?"

15 Then Jesus said to them,

"Be careful and guard against all kinds of greed. A man's life is not measured by the many things he owns."

Luke 12:16-23

16 Then Jesus used this story:

"There was a rich man who had some land, which grew a good crop of food. 17 The rich man thought to himself,

'What will I do? I have no place to keep all my crops.'

18 Then he said,

'I know what I will do. I will tear down my barns and build bigger ones! I will put all my grain and other goods together in my new barns. 19 Then I can say to myself, I have enough good things stored to last for many years. Rest, eat, drink, and enjoy life!'

20 "But God said to that man, 'Foolish man! Tonight you will die. So who will get those things you have prepared for yourself?'

21 "This is how it will be for anyone who stores things up only for himself and is not rich toward God."

Don't Worry

22 Jesus said to his followers,

"So I tell you, don't worry about the food you need to live. Don't worry about the clothes you need for your body. 23 Life is more important than food. And the body is more important than clothes.

24 "Look at the birds. They don't plant or harvest. They don't save food in houses or barns. But God takes care of them.

And you are worth much more than birds. 25 None of you can add any time to your life by worrying about it. 26 If you cannot do even the little things, then why worry about the big things? 27 Look at the wild flowers. See how they grow.

They don't work or make clothes for themselves. But I tell you that even Solomon, the great and rich king, was not dressed as beautifully

as one of these flowers. 28 God clothes the grass in the field like that. That grass is living today, but tomorrow it will be thrown into the fire. So you know how much more God will clothe you. Don't have so little faith! 29 Don't always think about what you will eat or what you will drink. Don't worry about it. 30 All the people in the world are trying to get those things. Your Father knows that you need them. 31 The thing you should seek is God's kingdom. Then all the other things you need will be given to you.

Don't Trust in Money

32 "Don't fear, little flock. Your Father wants to give you the kingdom. 33 Sell the things you have and give to the poor. Get for yourselves purses that don't wear out.

Get the treasure in heaven that never runs out. Thieves can't steal it in heaven, and moths can't destroy it. 34 Your heart will be where your treasure is.

Always Be Ready

35 "Be ready! Be dressed for service and have your lamps shining. 36 Be like servants who are waiting for their master to come home from a wedding party. The master comes and knocks. The servants immediately open the door for him. 37 Those servants will be blessed when their master comes home, because he sees that his servants are ready and waiting for him. I tell you the truth. The master will dress himself to serve and tell the servants to sit at the table. Then the master will serve them. 38 Those servants might have to wait until midnight or later for their master. But they will be happy when he comes in and finds them still waiting. 39 "Remember this: If the owner of the house knew what time a thief was coming, then the owner would not allow the thief to enter his house. 40 So you also must be ready! The Son of Man[d] will come at a time when you don't expect him!"

Who Is the Trusted Servant?

41 Peter said,

"Lord, did you tell this story for us or for all people?"

42 The Lord said,

"Who is the wise and trusted servant? Who is the servant the master trusts to give the other servants their food at the right time? 43 When the master comes and finds his servant doing the work he gave him, that servant will be very happy. 44 I tell you the truth. The master will choose that servant to take care of everything the master owns. 45 But what will happen if the servant is evil and thinks that his master will not come back soon? That servant will begin to beat the other servants, men and women. He will eat and drink and get drunk. 46 Then the master will come when that servant is not ready. It will be a time when the servant is not expecting him. Then the master will cut him in pieces and send him away to be with the others who don't obey.

47 "The servant who knows what his master wants but is not ready or does not do what the master wants will be beaten with many blows! 48 But the servant who does not know what his master wants and does things that should be punished will be beaten with few blows. Everyone who has been given much will be responsible for much. Much more will be expected from the one who has been given more."

Jesus Causes Division

49 Jesus continued speaking,

"I came to set fire to the world. I wish it were already burning! 50 I must be baptized with a different kind of baptism.ⁿ I feel very troubled until it is over. 51 Do you think that I came to give peace to the world? No! I came to divide the world! 52 From now on, a family with five people will be divided, three against two, and two against three. 53 A father and son will be divided: The son will be against his father. The father will be against his son. A mother and her daughter will be divided: The daughter will be against her mother. The mother will be against her daughter. A mother-in-law and her daughter-in-law will be divided: The daughter-in-law will be against her mother-in-law. The mother-in-law will be against her daughter-in-law."

Understanding the Times

54 Then Jesus said to the people,

"When you see clouds coming up in the west, you say, 'It's going to rain.' And soon it begins to rain. 55 When you feel the wind begin to blow from the south, you say, 'It will be a hot day.' And you are right. 56 Hypocrites!ᵈ You can understand the weather. Why don't you understand what is happening now?

Settle Your Problems

57 "Why can't you decide for yourselves what is right? 58 When someone is suing you, and you are going with him to court, try hard to settle it on the way. If you don't settle it, he may take you to the judge. The judge might turn you over to the officer. And the officer might throw you into jail. 59 You will not get out of there until they have taken everything you have."

12:50 I . . . baptism. Jesus was talking about the suffering he would soon go through.

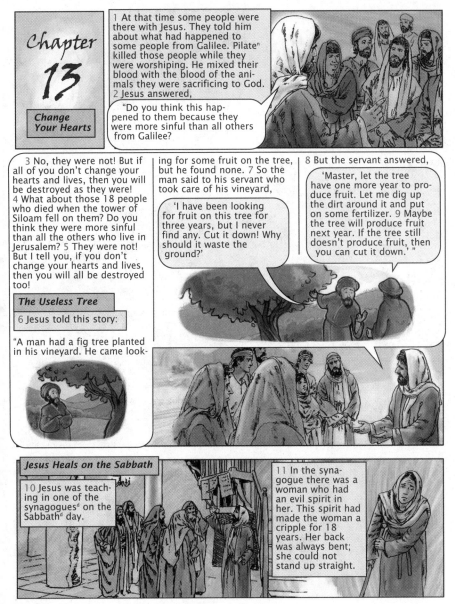

Chapter 13

Change Your Hearts

1 At that time some people were there with Jesus. They told him about what had happened to some people from Galilee. Pilate[n] killed those people while they were worshiping. He mixed their blood with the blood of the animals they were sacrificing to God. 2 Jesus answered,

"Do you think this happened to them because they were more sinful than all others from Galilee?

3 No, they were not! But if all of you don't change your hearts and lives, then you will be destroyed as they were! 4 What about those 18 people who died when the tower of Siloam fell on them? Do you think they were more sinful than all the others who live in Jerusalem? 5 They were not! But I tell you, if you don't change your hearts and lives, then you will all be destroyed too!

The Useless Tree

6 Jesus told this story:

"A man had a fig tree planted in his vineyard. He came looking for some fruit on the tree, but he found none. 7 So the man said to his servant who took care of his vineyard,

'I have been looking for fruit on this tree for three years, but I never find any. Cut it down! Why should it waste the ground?'

8 But the servant answered,

'Master, let the tree have one more year to produce fruit. Let me dig up the dirt around it and put on some fertilizer. 9 Maybe the tree will produce fruit next year. If the tree still doesn't produce fruit, then you can cut it down.' "

Jesus Heals on the Sabbath

10 Jesus was teaching in one of the synagogues[d] on the Sabbath[d] day.

11 In the synagogue there was a woman who had an evil spirit in her. This spirit had made the woman a cripple for 18 years. Her back was always bent; she could not stand up straight.

13:1 Pilate Pontius Pilate was the Roman governor of Judea from A.D. 26 to A.D. 36.

Luke 13:12-17

12 When Jesus saw her, he called her over and said,

"Woman, your sickness has left you!"

13 Jesus put his hands on her. Immediately she was able to stand up straight and began praising God.

14 The synagogue leader was angry because Jesus healed on the Sabbath day. He said to the people,

"There are six days for work. So come to be healed on one of those days. Don't come for healing on the Sabbath day."

15 The Lord answered,

"You people are hypocrites!d All of you untie your work animals and lead them to drink water every day—even on the Sabbath day! 16 This woman that I healed is our Jewish sister. But Satan has held her for 18 years. Surely it is not wrong for her to be freed from her sickness on a Sabbath day!"

17 When Jesus said this, all the men who were criticizing him were ashamed. And all the people were happy for the wonderful things Jesus was doing.

Stories of Mustard Seed and Yeast

18 Then Jesus said,

"What is God's kingdom like? What can I compare it with? 19 God's kingdom is like the seed of the mustard plant."

A man plants this seed in his garden. The seed grows and becomes a tree. The wild birds build nests on its branches."

20 Jesus said again,

"What can I compare God's kingdom with? 21 It is like yeast that a woman mixes into a big bowl of flour. The yeast makes all the dough rise."

The Narrow Door

22 Jesus was teaching in every town and village. He continued to travel toward Jerusalem. 23 Someone said to Jesus,

"Lord, how many people will be saved? Only a few?"

Jesus said,

24 "Try hard to enter through the narrow door that opens the way to heaven! Many people will try to enter there, but they will not be able.

25 A man gets up and closes the door of his house. You can stand outside and knock on the door. You can say,

'Sir, open the door for us!'

But he will answer,

'I don't know you! Where did you come from?'

13:19 mustard plant The seed is very small, but the plant grows taller than a man.

26 "Then you will say,

'We ate and drank with you. You taught in the streets of our town.'

27 But he will say to you,

'I don't know you! Where did you come from? Go away from me! All of you do evil!'

28 You will see Abraham, Isaac, Jacob, and all the prophets[d] in God's kingdom. But you will be thrown outside. Then you will cry and grind your teeth with pain. 29 People will come from the east, west, north, and south. They will sit down at the table in the kingdom of God.

30 Those who are last now will be first in the future. And those who are first now will be last in the future."

Jesus Will Die in Jerusalem

31 At that time some Phari-sees[d] came to Jesus and said,

"Go away from here! Herod wants to kill you!"

32 Jesus said to them,

"Go tell that fox Herod, 'Today and tomorrow I am forcing demons[d] out of people and finishing my work of healing. Then, on the third day, I will reach my goal.' 33 Yet I must be on my way today and tomorrow and the next day. Surely it cannot be right for a prophet[d] to be killed anywhere except in Jerusalem.

34 "Jerusalem, Jerusalem! You kill the prophets. You kill with stones those men that God has sent you. Many times I wanted to help your people. I wanted to gather them together as a hen gathers her chicks under her wings. But you did not let me. 35 Now your home will be left completely empty. I tell you, you will not see me again until that time when you will say, 'God bless the One who comes in the name of the Lord.' "[n]

13:35 'God . . . Lord.' Quotation from Psalm 118:26.

Chapter

14

Is It Right to Heal on the Sabbath?

1 On a Sabbath[d] day, Jesus went to the home of a leading Pharisee[d] to eat with him. The people there were all watching Jesus very closely. 2 A man with dropsy[n] was brought before Jesus. 3 Jesus said to the Pharisees and teachers of the law,

"Is it right or wrong to heal on the Sabbath day?"

4 But they would not answer his question.

So Jesus took the man, healed him, and sent him away.

5 Jesus said to the Pharisees and teachers of the law,

"If your son[n] or ox falls into a well on the Sabbath day, will you not pull him out quickly?"

6 And they could not answer him.

Don't Make Yourself Important

7 Then Jesus noticed that some of the guests were choosing the best places to sit. So Jesus told this story:

8 "When someone invites you to a wedding feast, don't take the most important seat. The host may have invited someone more important than you. 9 And if you are sitting in the most important seat, the host will come to you and say, 'Give this man your seat.' Then you will begin to move down to the last place. And you will be very embarrassed. 10 So when you are invited, go sit in a seat that is not important. Then the host will come to you and say, 'Friend, move up here to a more important place!' Then all the other guests will respect you. 11 Everyone who makes himself great will be made humble. But the person who makes himself humble will be made great."

14:2 **dropsy** A sickness that causes the body to swell larger and larger.
14:5 **son** Some Greek copies read "donkey."

Luke 14:12-21

12 Then Jesus said to the man who had invited him,

"When you give a lunch or a dinner, don't invite only your friends, brothers, relatives, and rich neighbors. At another time they will invite you to eat with them. Then you will have your reward. 13 Instead, when you give a feast, invite the poor, the crippled, the lame and the blind. 14 Then you will be blessed, because they cannot pay you back. They have nothing. But you will be rewarded when the good people rise from death."

15 One of the men sitting at the table with Jesus heard these things. The man said to Jesus,

"The people who will eat a meal in God's kingdom are blessed."

16 Jesus said to him,

"A man gave a big banquet and invited many people. 17 When it was time to eat, the man sent his servant to tell the guests,

'Come! Everything is ready.'

18 "But all the guests said they could not come. Each man made an excuse. The first one said,

'I have just bought a field, and I must go look at it. Please excuse me.'

19 Another man said,

'I have just bought five pairs of oxen; I must go and try them. out; please excuse me.'

20 A third man said,

'I just got married; I can't come.'

21 So the servant returned. He told his master what had happened. Then the master became angry and said,

'Go at once into the streets and alleys of the town. Bring in the poor, the crippled, the blind, and the lame.'

22 "Later the servant said to him,

'Master, I did what you told me to do, but we still have places for more people.'

23 The master said to the servant,

'Go out to the roads and country lanes. Tell the people there to come. I want my house to be full!

24 None of those men that I invited first will ever eat with me!' "

You Must First Plan

25 Large crowds were traveling with Jesus. He turned and said to them,

26 "If anyone comes to me but loves his father, mother, wife, children, brothers, or sisters more than he loves me, then he cannot be my follower. A person must love me more than he loves himself! 27 If anyone is not willing to die on a cross when he follows me, then he cannot be my follower.

28 If you wanted to build a tower, you would first sit down and decide how much it would cost. You must see if you have enough money to finish the job. 29 If you don't do that, you might begin the work, but you would not be able to finish. And if you could not finish it, then all who would see it would laugh at you.

30 They would say, 'This man began to build but was not able to finish!'
31 "If a king is going to fight against another king, first he will sit down and plan. If the king has only 10,000 men, he will plan to see if he is able to defeat the other king who has 20,000 men.

32 "If he cannot defeat the other king, then he will send some men to speak to the other king and ask for peace. 33 In the same way, you must give up everything you have to follow me. If you don't, you cannot be my follower!

Don't Lose Your Influence

34 "Salt is a good thing. But if the salt loses its salty taste, then it is worth nothing. You cannot make it salty again.

35 It is no good for the soil or for manure. People throw it away. "Let those with ears use them and listen!"

Chapter 15

A Lost Sheep and a Lost Coin

1 Many tax collectors and "sinners" came to listen to Jesus. 2 The Pharisees[d] and the teachers of the law began to complain:

"Look! This man welcomes sinners and even eats with them!"

3 Then Jesus told them this story:

4 "Suppose one of you has 100 sheep, but he loses 1 of them.

Then he will leave the other 99 sheep alone and go out and look for the lost sheep. The man will keep on searching for the lost sheep until he finds it.

5 And when he finds it, the man is very happy. He puts it on his shoulders

6 and goes home. He calls to his friends and neighbors and says,

'Be happy with me because I found my lost sheep!'

7 In the same way, I tell you there is much joy in heaven when 1 sinner changes his heart. There is more joy for that 1 sinner than there is for 99 good people who don't need to change.

8 "Suppose a woman has ten silver coins,ⁿ but she loses one of them. She will light a lamp and clean the house.

She will look carefully for the coin until she finds it.

9 And when she finds it, she will call her friends and neighbors and say,

'Be happy with me because I have found the coin that I lost!'

10 In the same way, there is joy before the angels of God when 1 sinner changes his heart."

The Son Who Left Home

11 Then Jesus said,

"A man had two sons.

12 The younger son said to his father,

'Give me my share of the property.'

So the father divided the property between his two sons. 13 Then the younger son gathered up all that was his and left.

He traveled far away to another country. There he wasted his money in foolish living.

14 He spent everything that he had. Soon after that, the land became very dry, and there was no rain. There was not enough food to eat anywhere in the country. The son was hungry and needed money. 15 So he got a job with one of the citizens there. The man sent

the son into the fields to feed pigs. 16 The son was so hungry that he was willing to eat the food the pigs were eating. But no one gave him anything. 17 The son realized that he had been very foolish. He thought,

'All of my father's servants have plenty of food. But I am here, almost dying with hunger.

18 I will leave and return to my father. I'll say to him: Father, I have sinned against God and against you. 19 I am not good enough to be called your son. But let me be like one of your servants.'

15:8 silver coins A Roman denarius. One coin was the average pay for one day's work.

73

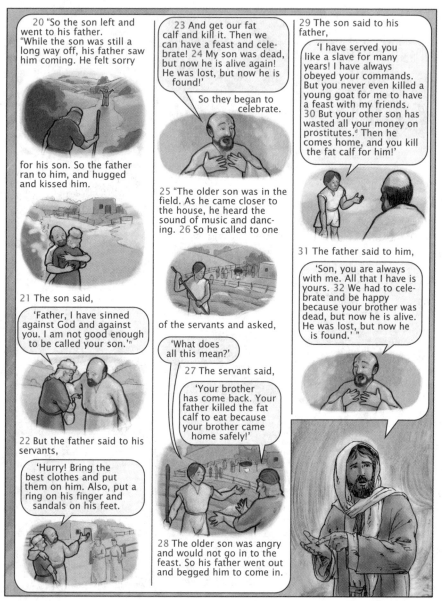

20 "So the son left and went to his father. "While the son was still a long way off, his father saw him coming. He felt sorry

for his son. So the father ran to him, and hugged and kissed him.

21 The son said,

'Father, I have sinned against God and against you. I am not good enough to be called your son.'ⁿ

22 But the father said to his servants,

'Hurry! Bring the best clothes and put them on him. Also, put a ring on his finger and sandals on his feet.

23 And get our fat calf and kill it. Then we can have a feast and celebrate! 24 My son was dead, but now he is alive again! He was lost, but now he is found!'

So they began to celebrate.

25 "The older son was in the field. As he came closer to the house, he heard the sound of music and dancing. 26 So he called to one

of the servants and asked,

'What does all this mean?'

27 The servant said,

'Your brother has come back. Your father killed the fat calf to eat because your brother came home safely!'

28 The older son was angry and would not go in to the feast. So his father went out and begged him to come in.

29 The son said to his father,

'I have served you like a slave for many years! I have always obeyed your commands. But you never even killed a young goat for me to have a feast with my friends. 30 But your other son has wasted all your money on prostitutes.ᵈ Then he comes home, and you kill the fat calf for him!'

31 The father said to him,

'Son, you are always with me. All that I have is yours. 32 We had to celebrate and be happy because your brother was dead, but now he is alive. He was lost, but now he is found.' "

15:21 son Some Greek copies continue, "But let me be like one of your servants" (see verse 19).

Chapter 16

True Wealth

1 Jesus also said to his followers,

"Once there was a rich man. He had a manager to take care of his business. Later, the rich man learned that his manager was cheating him. 2 So he called the manager in and said to him,

'I have heard bad things about you. Give me a report of what you have done with my money. You can't be my manager any longer!'

3 Later, the manager thought to himself,

'What will I do? My master is taking my job away from me! I am not strong enough to dig ditches. I am too proud to beg. 4 I know! I'll do something so that when I lose my job, people will welcome me into their homes.'

5 "So the manager called in everyone who owed the master any money. He said to the first man,

'How much do you owe my master?'

6 The man answered,

'I owe him 800 gallons of olive oil.'

The manager said to him,

'Here is your bill; sit down quickly and make the bill less. Write 400 gallons.'

7 Then the manager said to another man,

'How much do you owe my master?'

The man answered,

'I owe him 1,000 bushels of wheat.'

Then the manager said to him,

'Here is your bill; you can make it less. Write 800 bushels.'

8 Later, the master praised the dishonest manager for being smart. Yes, worldly people are smarter with their own kind than spiritual people are.

9 "I tell you, make friends for yourselves using worldly riches. Then, when those things are gone, you will be welcomed in that home that continues forever.

Luke 16:10-18

10 "Whoever can be trusted with small things can also be trusted with large things. Whoever is dishonest in little things will be dishonest in large things too. 11 If you cannot be trusted with worldly riches, then you will not be trusted with the true riches. 12 And if you cannot be trusted with the things that belong to someone else, then you will not be given things of your own.

13 "No servant can serve two masters. He will hate one master and love the other. Or he will follow one master and refuse to follow the other. You cannot serve both God and money."

God's Law Cannot Be Changed

14 The Pharisees[d] were listening to all these things. They made fun of Jesus because they all loved money. 15 Jesus said to them,

"You make yourselves look good in front of people. But God knows what is really in your hearts. The things that are important to people are worth nothing to God. 16 "God wanted the people to live by the law of Moses and the writings of the prophets.[d] But ever since John[n] came, the Good News[d] about the kingdom of God is being told. Now everyone is trying hard to get into the kingdom. 17 Even the smallest part of a letter in the law cannot be changed. It would be easier for heaven and earth to pass away.

Divorce and Remarriage

18 "If a man divorces his wife and marries another woman, he is guilty of adultery.[d] And the man who marries a divorced woman is also guilty of adultery."

16:16 John John the Baptist, who preached to people about Christ's coming (Matthew 3, Luke 3).

The Rich Man and Lazarus

19 Jesus said,

"There was a rich man who always dressed in the finest clothes. He lived in luxury every day. 20 There was also a very poor man named Lazarus, whose body was covered with sores. Lazarus was often placed at the rich man's gate. 21 He wanted to eat only the small pieces of food that fell from the rich man's table. And the dogs would come and lick his sores!

22 Later, Lazarus died. The angels took Lazarus and placed him in the arms of Abraham.[d]

The rich man died, too, and was buried.

23 But he was sent to where the dead are and had much pain. The rich man saw Abraham far away with Lazarus in his arms. 24 He called,

'Father Abraham, have mercy on me! Send Lazarus to me so that he can dip his finger in water and cool my tongue. I am suffering in this fire!'

25 But Abraham said,

'My child, remember when you lived? You had all the good things in life, but all the bad things happened to Lazarus. Now Lazarus is comforted here, and you are suffering.

26 Also, there is a big pit between you and us. No one can cross over to help you. And no one can leave there and come here.'

27 The rich man said,

'Then please send Lazarus to my father's house on earth! 28 I have five brothers. Lazarus could warn my brothers so that they will not come to this place of pain.'

29 But Abraham said,

'They have the law of Moses and the writings of the prophets[d] to read; let them learn from them!'

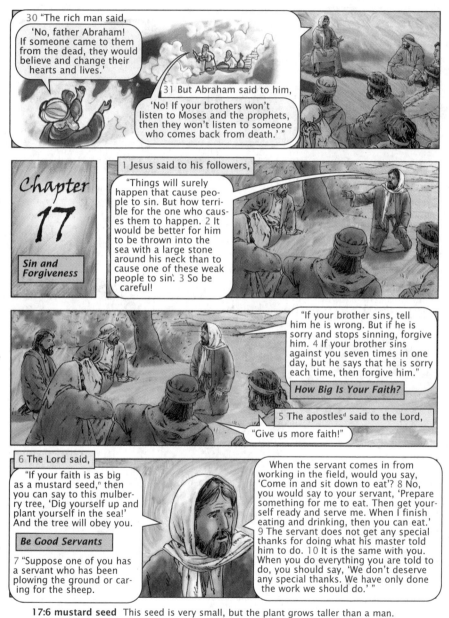

30 "The rich man said,

'No, father Abraham! If someone came to them from the dead, they would believe and change their hearts and lives.'

31 But Abraham said to him,

'No! If your brothers won't listen to Moses and the prophets, then they won't listen to someone who comes back from death.' "

Chapter 17

Sin and Forgiveness

1 Jesus said to his followers,

"Things will surely happen that cause people to sin. But how terrible for the one who causes them to happen. 2 It would be better for him to be thrown into the sea with a large stone around his neck than to cause one of these weak people to sin'. 3 So be careful!

"If your brother sins, tell him he is wrong. But if he is sorry and stops sinning, forgive him. 4 If your brother sins against you seven times in one day, but he says that he is sorry each time, then forgive him."

How Big Is Your Faith?

5 The apostles[d] said to the Lord,

"Give us more faith!"

6 The Lord said,

"If your faith is as big as a mustard seed,[n] then you can say to this mulberry tree, 'Dig yourself up and plant yourself in the sea!' And the tree will obey you.

Be Good Servants

7 "Suppose one of you has a servant who has been plowing the ground or caring for the sheep.

When the servant comes in from working in the field, would you say, 'Come in and sit down to eat'? 8 No, you would say to your servant, 'Prepare something for me to eat. Then get yourself ready and serve me. When I finish eating and drinking, then you can eat.' 9 The servant does not get any special thanks for doing what his master told him to do. 10 It is the same with you. When you do everything you are told to do, you should say, 'We don't deserve any special thanks. We have only done the work we should do.' "

17:6 mustard seed This seed is very small, but the plant grows taller than a man.

Be Thankful

11 Jesus was on his way to Jerusalem. Traveling from Galilee to Samaria, 12 he came into a small town. Ten men met him there. These men did not come close to Jesus, because they all had a harmful skin disease. 13 But they called to him,

"Jesus! Master! Please help us!"

14 When Jesus saw the men, he said,

"Go and show yourselves to the priests."[n]

While the ten men were going, they were healed.

15 When one of them saw that he was healed, he went back to Jesus. He praised God in a loud voice. 16 Then he bowed down at Jesus' feet and thanked him. (This man was a Samaritan.[d])

17 Jesus asked,

"Ten men were healed; where are the other nine? 18 Is this Samaritan the only one who came back to thank God?"

19 Then Jesus said to him,

"Stand up and go on your way. You were healed because you believed."

God's Kingdom Is Within You

20 Some of the Pharisees[d] asked Jesus,

"When will the kingdom of God come?"

Jesus answered,

"God's kingdom is coming, but not in a way that you will be able to see with your eyes. 21 People will not say, 'Look, God's kingdom is here!' or, 'There it is!' No, God's kingdom is within you."

17:14 show . . . priests The law of Moses said a priest must say when a Jew with a harmful skin disease became well.

22 Then Jesus said to his followers,

"The time will come when you will want very much to see one of the days of the Son of Man.[d] But you will not be able to see it. 23 People will say to you, 'Look, there he is!' or, 'Look, here he is!' Stay where you are; don't go away and search.

When Jesus Comes Again

24 "The Son of Man[d] will come again. On the day he comes he will shine like lightning, which flashes across the sky and lights it up from one side to the other. 25 But first, the Son of Man must suffer many things and be rejected by the people of this time. 26 When the Son of Man comes again, it will be as it was when Noah lived. 27 In the time of Noah, people were eating, drinking, and getting married even on the day when Noah entered the boat. Then the flood came and killed all the people. 28 It will be the same as during the time of Lot. Those people were eating, drinking, buying, selling, planting, and building. 29 They were doing these things even on the day Lot left Sodom.[n] Then fire and sulfur rained down from the sky and killed them all. 30 This is exactly how it will be when the Son of Man comes again.

31 "On that day, if a man is on his roof, he will not have time to go inside and get his things. If a man is in the field, he cannot go back home. 32 Remember what happened to Lot's wife?[n] 33 Whoever tries to keep his life will give up true life. But whoever gives up his life will have true life. 34 At the time when I come again, there may be two people sleeping in one bed. One will be taken and the other will be left. 35 There may be two women grinding grain together. One will be taken and the other will be left. 36 [Two men will be in the same field. One man will be taken, but the other man will be left behind.]"[n]

37 The followers asked Jesus,

"Where will this be, Lord?"

Jesus answered,

"People can always find a dead body by looking for the vultures."

Chapter
18

17:29 **Sodom** City that God destroyed because the people were so evil. **17:32 Lot's wife** A story about what happened to Lot's wife is found in Genesis 19:15-17, 26. **17:36 Two . . . behind.** Some Greek copies do not contain the bracketed text.

God Will Answer His People

1 Then Jesus used this story to teach his followers that they should always pray and never lose hope.

2 "Once there was a judge in a town. He did not care about God. He also did not care what people thought about him. 3 In that same town there was a widow who kept coming to this judge. She said,

'There is a man who is not being fair to me. Give me my rights!'

4 But the judge did not want to help the widow. After a long time, he thought to himself,

'I don't care about God. And I don't care about what people think. 5 But this widow is bothering me. I will see that she gets her rights, or she will bother me until I am worn out!' "

6 The Lord said,

"Listen to what the bad judge said. 7 God's people cry to him night and day. God will always give them what is right, and he will not be slow to answer them. 8 I tell you, God will help his people quickly! But when the Son of Man[d] comes again, will he find those on earth who believe in him?"

Being Right with God

9 There were some people who thought that they were very good and looked down on everyone else. Jesus used this story to teach them:

10 "One day there was a Pharisee[d] and a tax collector. Both went to the Temple[d] to pray.

11 The Pharisee stood alone, away from the tax collector. When the Pharisee prayed, he said,

'God, I thank you that I am not as bad as other people. I am not like men who steal, cheat, or take part in adultery.[d] I thank you that I am better than this tax collector. 12 I give up eating[n] twice a week, and I give one-tenth of everything I earn!'

13 "The tax collector stood at a distance. When he prayed, he would not even look up to heaven. He beat on his chest because he was so sad. He said,

'God, have mercy on me. I am a sinner!'

14 I tell you, when this man went home, he was right with God. But the Pharisee was not right with God. Everyone who makes himself great will be made humble. But everyone who makes himself humble will be made great."

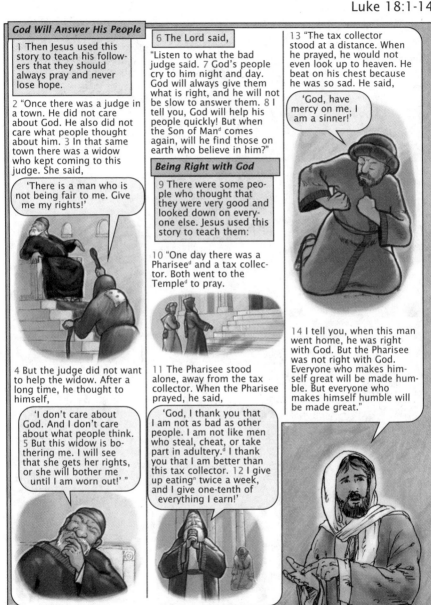

18:12 give up eating This is called "fasting." The people would give up eating for a special time of prayer and worship to God. It was also done to show sadness.

18:20 'You . . . mother.' Quotation from Exodus 20:12-16; Deuteronomy 5:16-20.

29 Jesus said,

"I tell you the truth. Everyone who has left his house, wife, brothers, parents, or children for God's kingdom 30 will get much more than he left. He will receive many times more in this life. And after he dies, he will live with God forever."

Jesus Will Rise from Death

31 Then Jesus talked to the 12 apostles[d] alone. He said to them,

"Listen! We are going to Jerusalem. Everything that God told the prophets[d] to write about the Son of Man d will happen! 32 He will be turned over to the non-Jewish people. They will laugh at him, insult him, and spit on him. 33 They will beat him with whips and then kill him. But on the third day after his death, he will rise to life again."

34 The apostles tried to understand this, but they could not; the meaning was hidden from them.

Jesus Heals a Blind Man

35 Jesus was coming near the city of Jericho. There was a blind man sitting beside the road, begging for money. 36 When he heard the people coming down the road,

he asked,

"What is happening?"

37 They told him,

"Jesus, the one from Nazareth, is coming here."

38 The blind man cried out,

"Jesus, Son of David![d] Please help me!"

39 The people who were in front, leading the group, told the blind man to be quiet. But the blind man shouted more and more,

"Son of David, please help me!"

40 Jesus stopped and said,

"Bring the blind man to me!"

When he came near, Jesus asked him,

41 "What do you want me to do for you?"

He said,

"Lord, I want to see again."

42 Jesus said to him,

"Then see! You are healed because you believed."

43 At once the man was able to see,

and he followed Jesus, thanking God. All the people who saw this praised God.

Chapter

19

Zacchaeus

1 Jesus was going through the city of Jericho. 2 In Jericho there was a man named Zacchaeus. He was a wealthy, very important tax collector. 3 He wanted to see who Jesus was, but he was too short to see above the crowd. 4 He ran ahead to a place where he knew Jesus would come. He climbed a sycamore tree so he could see Jesus. 5 When Jesus came to that place, he looked up and saw Zacchaeus in the tree. He said to him,

"Zacchaeus, hurry and come down! I must stay at your house today."

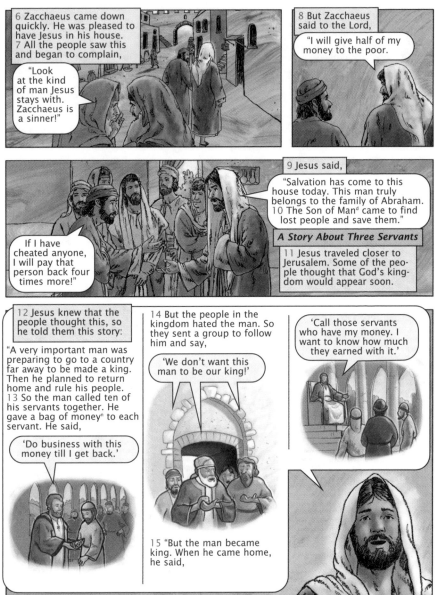

6 Zacchaeus came down quickly. He was pleased to have Jesus in his house. 7 All the people saw this and began to complain,

"Look at the kind of man Jesus stays with. Zacchaeus is a sinner!"

8 But Zacchaeus said to the Lord,

"I will give half of my money to the poor.

9 Jesus said,

"Salvation has come to this house today. This man truly belongs to the family of Abraham. 10 The Son of Man[d] came to find lost people and save them."

If I have cheated anyone, I will pay that person back four times more!"

A Story About Three Servants

11 Jesus traveled closer to Jerusalem. Some of the people thought that God's kingdom would appear soon.

12 Jesus knew that the people thought this, so he told them this story:

"A very important man was preparing to go to a country far away to be made a king. Then he planned to return home and rule his people. 13 So the man called ten of his servants together. He gave a bag of money[n] to each servant. He said,

'Do business with this money till I get back.'

14 But the people in the kingdom hated the man. So they sent a group to follow him and say,

'We don't want this man to be our king!'

15 "But the man became king. When he came home, he said,

'Call those servants who have my money. I want to know how much they earned with it.'

19:13 bag of money One bag of money was a Greek "mina." One mina was enough money to pay a person for working three months.

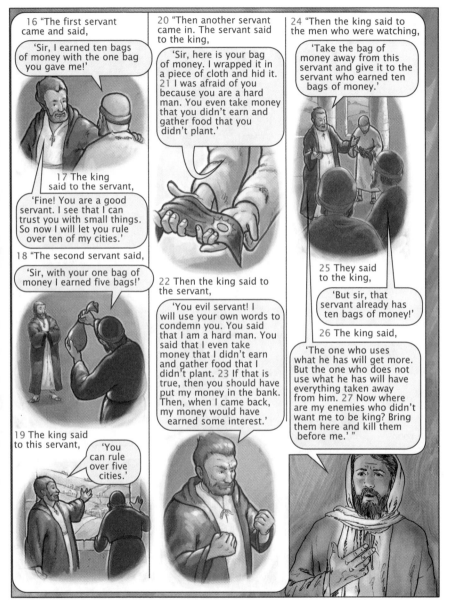

16 "The first servant came and said,

'Sir, I earned ten bags of money with the one bag you gave me!'

17 The king said to the servant,

'Fine! You are a good servant. I see that I can trust you with small things. So now I will let you rule over ten of my cities.'

18 "The second servant said,

'Sir, with your one bag of money I earned five bags!'

19 The king said to this servant,

'You can rule over five cities.'

20 "Then another servant came in. The servant said to the king,

'Sir, here is your bag of money. I wrapped it in a piece of cloth and hid it. 21 I was afraid of you because you are a hard man. You even take money that you didn't earn and gather food that you didn't plant.'

22 Then the king said to the servant,

'You evil servant! I will use your own words to condemn you. You said that I am a hard man. You said that I even take money that I didn't earn and gather food that I didn't plant. 23 If that is true, then you should have put my money in the bank. Then, when I came back, my money would have earned some interest.'

24 "Then the king said to the men who were watching,

'Take the bag of money away from this servant and give it to the servant who earned ten bags of money.'

25 They said to the king,

'But sir, that servant already has ten bags of money!'

26 The king said,

'The one who uses what he has will get more. But the one who does not use what he has will have everything taken away from him. 27 Now where are my enemies who didn't want me to be king? Bring them here and kill them before me.' "

Jesus Enters Jerusalem as a King

28 After Jesus said this, he went on toward Jerusalem. 29 Jesus came near Bethphage and Bethany, towns near the hill called the Mount of Olives.[d]

Then he sent out two of his followers. 30 He said,

"Go into the town you can see there. When you enter it, you will find a colt tied there. No one has ever ridden this colt. Untie it, and bring it here to me. 31 If anyone asks you why you are taking it, say, 'The Master needs it.'"

32 The two followers went into town. They found the colt just as Jesus told them.

33 The followers untied it, but the owners of the colt came out. They asked the followers,

"Why are you untying our colt?"

34 The followers answered,

"The Master needs it."

35 So they brought it to Jesus. They threw their coats on the colt's back and put Jesus on it.

36 As Jesus rode toward Jerusalem,

the followers spread their coats on the road before him.

37 Jesus was coming close to Jerusalem. He was already near the bottom of the Mount of Olives. The whole crowd of followers was very happy. They began shouting praise to God for all the powerful works they had seen. They said,

38 "God bless the king who comes in the name of the Lord! There is peace in heaven and glory to God!"
Psalm 118:26.

39 Some of the Pharisees[d] said to Jesus,

"Teacher, tell your followers not to say these things!"

40 But Jesus answered,

"I tell you, if my followers don't say these things, then the stones will cry out."

Jesus Cries for Jerusalem

41 Jesus came near Jerusalem. He saw the city and began to cry for it. 42 Jesus said to Jerusalem,

"I wish you knew today what would bring you peace! But you can't know it, because it is hidden from you. 43 A time is coming when your enemies will build a wall around you and will hold you in on all sides. 44 They will destroy you and all your people. Not one stone of your buildings will be left on another. All this will happen because you did not know the time when God came to save you."

Jesus Goes to the Temple

45 Jesus went into the Temple.[d] He began to throw out the people who were selling things there. 46 He said,

"It is written in the Scriptures,[d] 'My Temple will be a house where people will pray.'[n] But you have changed it into a 'hideout for robbers'!"[n]

47 Jesus taught in the Temple every day. The leading priests, the teachers of the law, and some of the leaders of the people wanted to kill Jesus. 48 But all the people were listening closely to him and were interested in all the things he said. So the leading priests, the teachers of the law, and the leaders did not know how they could kill him.

Chapter 20

The Leaders Question Jesus

1 One day Jesus was in the Temple,[d] teaching the people and telling them the Good News.[d] The leading priests, teachers of the law, and Jewish elders came up to talk with him. 2 They said,

"Tell us! What authority do you have to do these things? Who gave you this authority?"

3 Jesus answered,

"I will ask you a question too. Tell me: 4 When John baptized people, did that come from God or from man?"

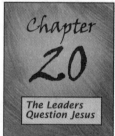

19:46 'My Temple . . . pray.' Quotation from Isaiah 56:7.
19:46 'hideout for robbers' Quotation from Jeremiah 7:11.

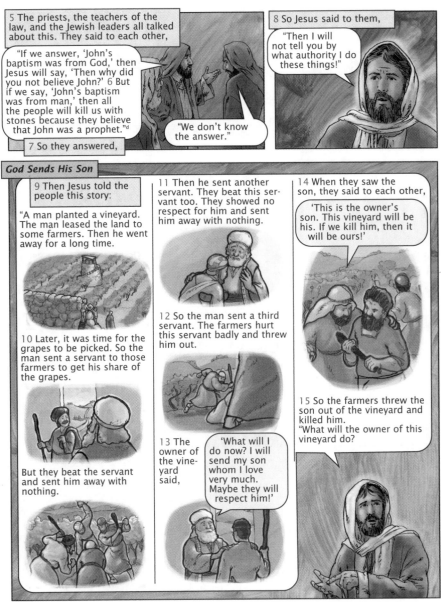

5 The priests, the teachers of the law, and the Jewish leaders all talked about this. They said to each other,

"If we answer, 'John's baptism was from God,' then Jesus will say, 'Then why did you not believe John?' 6 But if we say, 'John's baptism was from man,' then all the people will kill us with stones because they believe that John was a prophet."[d]

7 So they answered,

"We don't know the answer."

8 So Jesus said to them,

"Then I will not tell you by what authority I do these things!"

God Sends His Son

9 Then Jesus told the people this story:

"A man planted a vineyard. The man leased the land to some farmers. Then he went away for a long time.

10 Later, it was time for the grapes to be picked. So the man sent a servant to those farmers to get his share of the grapes.

But they beat the servant and sent him away with nothing.

11 Then he sent another servant. They beat this servant too. They showed no respect for him and sent him away with nothing.

12 So the man sent a third servant. The farmers hurt this servant badly and threw him out.

13 The owner of the vineyard said,

'What will I do now? I will send my son whom I love very much. Maybe they will respect him!'

14 When they saw the son, they said to each other,

'This is the owner's son. This vineyard will be his. If we kill him, then it will be ours!'

15 So the farmers threw the son out of the vineyard and killed him.
"What will the owner of this vineyard do?

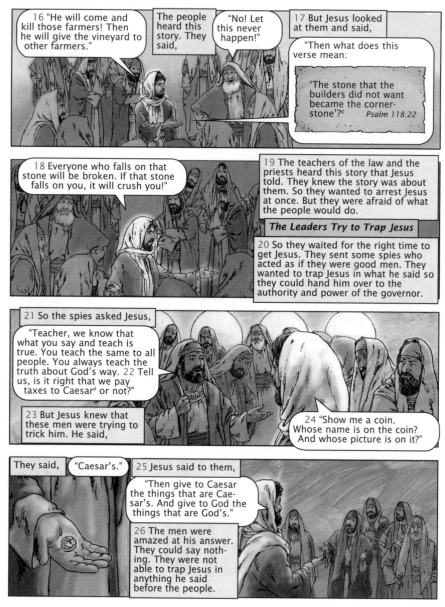

16 "He will come and kill those farmers! Then he will give the vineyard to other farmers."

The people heard this story. They said,

"No! Let this never happen!"

17 But Jesus looked at them and said,

"Then what does this verse mean:

'The stone that the builders did not want became the corner-stone'?[d] *Psalm 118:22*

18 Everyone who falls on that stone will be broken. If that stone falls on you, it will crush you!"

19 The teachers of the law and the priests heard this story that Jesus told. They knew the story was about them. So they wanted to arrest Jesus at once. But they were afraid of what the people would do.

The Leaders Try to Trap Jesus

20 So they waited for the right time to get Jesus. They sent some spies who acted as if they were good men. They wanted to trap Jesus in what he said so they could hand him over to the authority and power of the governor.

21 So the spies asked Jesus,

"Teacher, we know that what you say and teach is true. You teach the same to all people. You always teach the truth about God's way. 22 Tell us, is it right that we pay taxes to Caesar[d] or not?"

23 But Jesus knew that these men were trying to trick him. He said,

24 "Show me a coin. Whose name is on the coin? And whose picture is on it?"

They said, "Caesar's." 25 Jesus said to them,

"Then give to Caesar the things that are Caesar's. And give to God the things that are God's."

26 The men were amazed at his answer. They could say nothing. They were not able to trap Jesus in anything he said before the people.

Sadducees Try to Trick Jesus

27 Some Sadducees[d] came to Jesus. (Sadducees believe that people will not rise from death.) They asked,

28 "Teacher, Moses wrote that a man's brother might die. He leaves a wife but no children. Then that man must marry the widow and have children for his dead brother. 29 One time there were seven brothers. The first brother married, but died. He had no children. 30 Then the second brother married the widow, and he died. 31 And the third brother married the widow, and he died. The same thing happened with all the other brothers. They all died and had no children. 32 The woman was the last to die. 33 But all seven brothers married her. So when people rise from death, whose wife will the woman be?"

34 Jesus said to the Sadducees,

"On earth, people marry each other. 35 But those who will be worthy to be raised from death and live again will not marry. 36 In that life they are like angels and cannot die. They are children of God, because they have been raised from death. 37 Moses clearly showed that the dead are raised to life. When Moses wrote about the burning bush,[n] he said that the Lord is 'the God of Abraham, the God of Isaac, and the God of Jacob.'[n] 38 God is the God of living people, not dead people. All people are alive to God."

39 Some of the teachers of the law said,

"Teacher, your answer was good."

40 No one was brave enough to ask him another question.

Is the Christ the Son of David?

41 Then Jesus said,

"Why do people say that the Christ[d] is the Son of David?[d] 42 In the book of Psalms, David himself says:

'The Lord said to my Lord: Sit by me at my right side, 43 until I put your enemies under your control.'[n]

Psalm 110:1

44 David calls the Christ 'Lord.' But the Christ is also the son of David. How can both these things be true?"

Jesus Accuses the Leaders

45 While all the people were listening, Jesus said to his followers,

46 "Be careful of the teachers of the law.

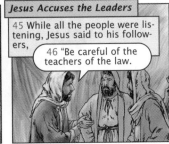

20:37 **burning bush** Read Exodus 3:1-12 in the Old Testament.
20:37 **'the God of . . . Jacob'** These words are taken from Exodus 3:6.
20:43 **until . . . control** Literally, "until I make your enemies a footstool for your feet."

93

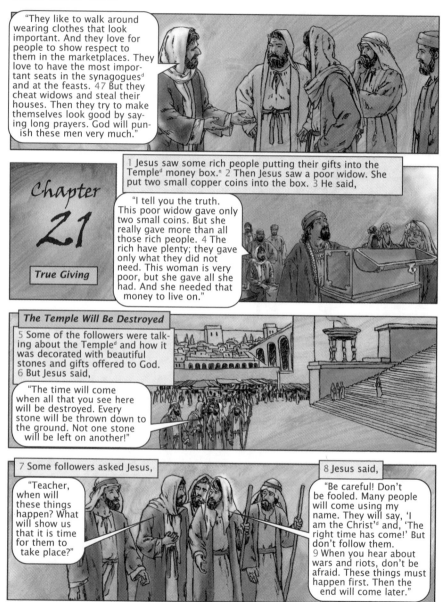

"They like to walk around wearing clothes that look important. And they love for people to show respect to them in the marketplaces. They love to have the most important seats in the synagogues[d] and at the feasts. 47 But they cheat widows and steal their houses. Then they try to make themselves look good by saying long prayers. God will punish these men very much."

Chapter 21

True Giving

1 Jesus saw some rich people putting their gifts into the Temple[d] money box.[n] 2 Then Jesus saw a poor widow. She put two small copper coins into the box. 3 He said,

"I tell you the truth. This poor widow gave only two small coins. But she really gave more than all those rich people. 4 The rich have plenty; they gave only what they did not need. This woman is very poor, but she gave all she had. And she needed that money to live on."

The Temple Will Be Destroyed

5 Some of the followers were talking about the Temple[d] and how it was decorated with beautiful stones and gifts offered to God. 6 But Jesus said,

"The time will come when all that you see here will be destroyed. Every stone will be thrown down to the ground. Not one stone will be left on another!"

7 Some followers asked Jesus,

"Teacher, when will these things happen? What will show us that it is time for them to take place?"

8 Jesus said,

"Be careful! Don't be fooled. Many people will come using my name. They will say, 'I am the Christ'[d] and, 'The right time has come!' But don't follow them. 9 When you hear about wars and riots, don't be afraid. These things must happen first. Then the end will come later."

21:1 **money box** A special box in the Jewish place for worship where people put their gifts to God.

10 Then he said to them,

"Nations will fight against other nations. Kingdoms will fight against other kingdoms. 11 There will be great earthquakes, sicknesses, and other terrible things in many places. In some places there will be no food for the people to eat. Fearful events and great signs will come from heaven.

12 "But before all these things happen, people will arrest you and treat you cruelly. They will judge you in their synagogues[d] and put you in jail. You will be forced to stand before kings and governors. They will do all these things to you because you follow me. 13 But this will give you an opportunity to tell about me. 14 Don't worry about what you will say. 15 I will give you the wisdom to say things so that none of your enemies will be able to show that you are wrong. 16 Even your parents, brothers, relatives and friends will turn against you. They will kill some of you. 17 All people will hate you because you follow me. 18 But none of these things can really harm you. 19 You will save yourselves by continuing strong in your faith through all these things.

Jerusalem Will Be Destroyed

20 "When you see armies all around Jerusalem, then you will know that it will soon be destroyed. 21 At that time, the people in Judea should run away to the mountains. The people in Jerusalem must get out. If you are near the city, don't go in!

22 These are the days of punishment to make come true all that is written in the Scriptures.[d] 23 At that time, it will be hard for women who are pregnant or have nursing babies! Great trouble will come upon this land, and God will be angry with these people. 24 Some will be killed by the sword and taken as prisoners to all nations. Jerusalem will be crushed by non-Jewish people until their time is over.

Don't Fear

25 "Amazing things will happen to the sun, moon, and stars. On earth, nations will be afraid because of the roar and fury of the sea. They will not know what to do.

Luke 21:26-38

26 "People will be so afraid they will faint. They will wonder what is happening to the whole world. Everything in the sky will be changed. 27 Then people will see the Son of Man[d] coming in a cloud with power and great glory. 28 When these things begin to happen, don't fear. Look up and hold your heads high because the time when God will free you is near!"

My Words Will Live Forever

29 Then Jesus told this story:

"Look at the fig tree and all the other trees. 30 When their leaves appear, you know that summer is near. 31 In the same way, when you see all these things happening, then you will know that God's kingdom is coming very soon.

32 "I tell you the truth. All these things will happen while the people of this time are still living! 33 The whole world, earth and sky, will be destroyed; but the words I have said will never be destroyed!

Be Ready All the Time

34 "Be careful! Don't spend your time feasting and drinking. Or don't be too busy with worldly things. If you do that, you will not be able to think straight. And then that day might come when you are not ready. 35 It will close like a trap on all people on earth. 36 So be ready all the time. Pray that you will be strong enough to escape all these things that will happen. And pray that you will be able to stand before the Son of Man."[d]

37 During the day, Jesus taught the people in the Temple.[d] At night he went out of the city and stayed on the Mount of Olives.[d]

38 Every morning all the people got up early to go to the Temple to listen to him.

Chapter 22

Plans to Kill Jesus

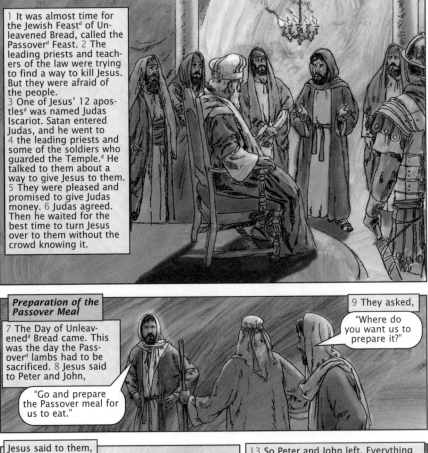

1 It was almost time for the Jewish Feast[d] of Unleavened Bread, called the Passover[d] Feast. 2 The leading priests and teachers of the law were trying to find a way to kill Jesus. But they were afraid of the people.
3 One of Jesus' 12 apostles[d] was named Judas Iscariot. Satan entered Judas, and he went to 4 the leading priests and some of the soldiers who guarded the Temple.[d] He talked to them about a way to give Jesus to them. 5 They were pleased and promised to give Judas money. 6 Judas agreed. Then he waited for the best time to turn Jesus over to them without the crowd knowing it.

Preparation of the Passover Meal

7 The Day of Unleavened[d] Bread came. This was the day the Passover[d] lambs had to be sacrificed. 8 Jesus said to Peter and John,

"Go and prepare the Passover meal for us to eat."

9 They asked,

"Where do you want us to prepare it?"

Jesus said to them,

10 "Listen! After you go into the city, you will see a man carrying a jar of water. Follow him into the house that he enters. 11 Tell the person who owns that house, 'The Teacher asks that you please show us the room where he and his followers may eat the Passover meal.' 12 Then he will show you a large room upstairs. This room is ready for you. Prepare the Passover meal there.'

13 So Peter and John left. Everything happened as Jesus had said. So they prepared the Passover meal.

Luke 22:14-20

22:18 **fruit of the vine** Product of the grapevine; this may also be translated "wine."
22:19 **body** Some Greek copies do not have the rest of verse 19 or verse 20.

Who Will Turn Against Jesus?

21 Jesus said,

"One of you will turn against me. His hand is by my hand on the table. 22 The Son of Man[d] will do what God has planned. But how terrible it will be for that man who gives the Son of Man to be killed."

23 Then the apostles[d] asked each other,

"Which one of us would do that to Jesus?"

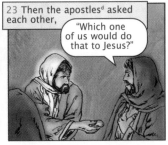

Be Like a Servant

24 Then the apostles[d] began to argue about which one of them was the most important. 25 But Jesus said to them,

"The kings of the world rule over their people. Men who have authority over others are called 'very important.' 26 But you must not be like that. The greatest among you should be like the youngest, and the leader should be like the servant. 27 Who is more important: the one sitting at the table or the one serving him? You think the one at the table is more important. But I am like a servant among you! 28 "You men have stayed with me through many struggles. 29 My Father has given me the power to rule. I also give you authority to rule with me. 30 You will eat and drink at my table in my kingdom. You will sit on thrones and judge the 12 tribes[d] of Israel.

Luke 22:31-40

Don't Lose Your Faith

31 "Satan has asked to test all of you as a farmer tests his wheat. Simon, Simon, 32 I have prayed that you will not lose your faith! Help your brothers be stronger when you come back to me."

33 But Peter said to Jesus,

"Lord, I am ready to go to prison with you. I will even die with you!"

34 But Jesus said,

"Peter, before the rooster crows tonight, you will say you don't know me. You will say this three times!"

Be Ready for Trouble

35 Then Jesus said to the apostles,[d]

"When I sent you out without money, a bag, or sandals, did you need anything?"

They said, "No."

36 He said to them,

"But now if you have money or a bag, carry that with you. If you don't have a sword, sell your coat and buy one. 37 The Scripture[d] says, 'He was treated like a criminal.'[n] This scripture must have its full meaning. It was written about me, and it is happening now."

38 The followers said,

"Look, Lord, here are two swords!"

He said to them,

"That's enough."

Jesus Prays Alone

39-40 Jesus left the city and went to the Mount of Olives.[d] His followers went with him. (Jesus went there often.) He said to his followers,

22:37 'He . . . criminal.' Quotation from Isaiah 53:12.

"Pray for strength against temptation."

41 Then Jesus went about a stone's throw away from them. He kneeled down and prayed,

42 "Father, if it is what you want, then let me not have this cup[n] of suffering. But do what you want, not what I want."

43 Then an angel from heaven appeared to him to help him.

44 Jesus was full of pain; he prayed even more. Sweat dripped from his face as if he were bleeding. 45 When he finished praying, he went to his followers. They were asleep. (Their sadness had made them very tired.)

46 Jesus said to them,

"Why are you sleeping? Get up and pray for strength against temptation."

Jesus Is Arrested

47 While Jesus was speaking, a crowd came up. One of the 12 apostles[d] was leading them. He was Judas. He came close to Jesus so that he could kiss him.

48 But Jesus said to him,

"Judas, are you using the kiss to give the Son of Man[d] to his enemies?"

49 The followers of Jesus were standing there too. They saw what was happening. They said to Jesus,

"Lord, should we use our swords?"

50 And one of them did use his sword. He cut off the right ear of the servant of the high priest.

22:42 cup Jesus is talking about the bad things that will happen to him. Accepting these things will be hard, like drinking a cup of something that tastes very bitter.

51 Jesus said, "Stop!"

Then he touched the servant's ear and healed him.
52 Those who came to arrest Jesus were the leading priests, the soldiers who guarded the Temple,[d] and the Jewish elders. Jesus said to them,

"Why did you come out here with swords and sticks? Do you think I am a criminal? 53 I was with you every day in the Temple. Why didn't you try to arrest me there? But this is your time—the time when darkness rules."

Peter Says He Doesn't Know Jesus

54 They arrested Jesus and took him away. They brought him into the house of the high priest. Peter followed them, but he did not go near Jesus.

55 The soldiers started a fire in the middle of the courtyard and sat together. Peter sat with them.

56 A servant girl saw Peter sitting there near the light. She looked closely at Peter's face and said,

"This man was also with him!"

57 But Peter said this was not true. He said,

"Girl, I don't know him."

58 A short time later, another person saw Peter and said,

"You are also one of them."

But Peter said,

"Man, I am not!"

59 About an hour later, another man insisted,

"It is true! This man was with him. He is from Galilee!"

60 But Peter said,

"Man, I don't know what you are talking about!"

Immediately, while Peter was still speaking, a rooster crowed. 61 Then the Lord turned and looked straight at Peter. And Peter remembered what the Lord had said:

"Before the rooster crows tonight, you will say three times that you don't know me."

62 Then Peter went outside and cried with much pain in his heart.

The People Laugh at Jesus

63-64 Some men were guarding Jesus. They made fun of him like this: They covered his eyes so that he could not see them. Then they hit him and said,

"Prove that you are a prophet,ᵈ and tell us who hit you!"

65 The men said many cruel things to Jesus.

Jesus Before the Leaders

66 When day came, the elders of the people, the leading priests, and the teachers of the law came together. They led Jesus away to their highest court. 67 They said,

"If you are the Christ,ᵈ then tell us that you are!"

Jesus said to them,

"If I tell you I am the Christ, you will not believe me. 68 And if I ask you, you will not answer. 69 But beginning now, the Son of Manᵈ will sit at the right hand of the powerful God."

70 They all said,

"Then are you the Son of God?"

Jesus said to them,

"Yes, you are right when you say that I am."

71 They said,

"Why do we need witnesses now? We ourselves heard him say this!"

Luke 23:1-10

Chapter 23

Governor Pilate Questions Jesus

1 Then the whole group stood up and led Jesus to Pilate.[n] 2 They began to accuse Jesus. They told Pilate,

"We caught this man telling things that were confusing our people. He says that we should not pay taxes to Caesar.[d] He calls himself the Christ,[d] a king."

3 Pilate asked Jesus,

"Are you the king of the Jews?"

Jesus answered,

"Yes, that is right."

4 Pilate said to the leading priests and the people,

"I find nothing wrong with this man."

5 They said again and again,

"But Jesus is making trouble with the people! He teaches all around Judea. He began in Galilee, and now he is here!"

Pilate Sends Jesus to Herod

6 Pilate heard this and asked if Jesus was from Galilee. 7 If so, Jesus was under Herod's authority. Herod was in Jerusalem at that time; so Pilate sent Jesus to him. 8 When Herod saw Jesus, he was very glad. He had heard about Jesus and had wanted to meet him for a long time. Herod was hoping to see Jesus work a miracle.[d] 9 Herod asked Jesus many questions, but Jesus said nothing. 10 The leading priests and teachers of the law were standing there. They were shouting things against Jesus.

23:1 Pilate Pontius Pilate was the Roman governor of Judea from A.D. 26 to A.D. 36.

11 Then Herod and his soldiers made fun of Jesus. They dressed him in a kingly robe and then sent him back to Pilate.

12 In the past, Pilate and Herod had always been enemies. But on that day they became friends.

Jesus Must Die

13 Pilate called all the people together with the leading priests and the Jewish leaders. 14 He said to them,

"You brought this man to me. You said that he was making trouble among the people. But I have questioned him before you all, and I have not found him guilty of the things you say.

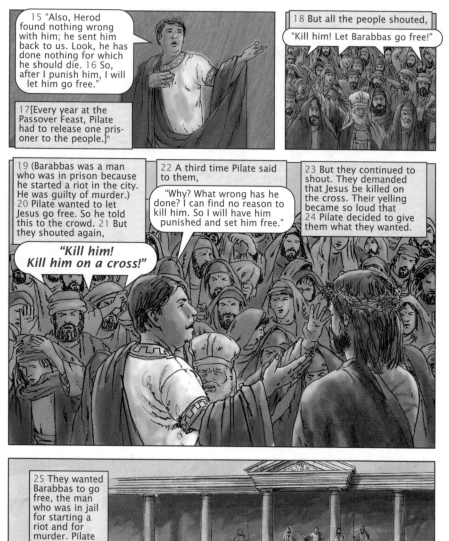

15 "Also, Herod found nothing wrong with him; he sent him back to us. Look, he has done nothing for which he should die. 16 So, after I punish him, I will let him go free."

17[Every year at the Passover Feast, Pilate had to release one prisoner to the people.]ⁿ

18 But all the people shouted,

"Kill him! Let Barabbas go free!"

19 (Barabbas was a man who was in prison because he started a riot in the city. He was guilty of murder.) 20 Pilate wanted to let Jesus go free. So he told this to the crowd. 21 But they shouted again,

22 A third time Pilate said to them,

"Why? What wrong has he done? I can find no reason to kill him. So I will have him punished and set him free."

23 But they continued to shout. They demanded that Jesus be killed on the cross. Their yelling became so loud that 24 Pilate decided to give them what they wanted.

"Kill him! Kill him on a cross!"

25 They wanted Barabbas to go free, the man who was in jail for starting a riot and for murder. Pilate let Barabbas go free and gave Jesus to them to be killed.

23:17 Every . . . people. Some Greek copies do not contain the bracketed text.

106

Jesus Is Killed on a Cross

26 The soldiers led Jesus away. At that time, there was a man coming into the city from the fields. His name was Simon, and he was from the city of Cyrene. The soldiers forced Simon to carry Jesus' cross and walk behind him.
27 A large crowd of people was following Jesus. Some of the women were sad and crying. 28 But Jesus turned and said to them,

"Women of Jerusalem, don't cry for me. Cry for yourselves and for your children too! 29 The time is coming when people will say, 'Happy are the women who cannot have children! Happy are the women who have no babies to nurse.'
30 Then people will say to the mountains, 'Fall on us!' And they will say to the hills, 'Cover us!'
31 If they act like this now when life is good, what will happen when bad times come?'"[n]

32 There were also two criminals led out with Jesus to be killed. 33 Jesus and the two criminals were taken to a place called the Skull. There the soldiers nailed Jesus to his cross. They also nailed the criminals to their crosses, one beside Jesus on the right and the other beside Jesus on the left.

23:31 If . . . come? Literally, "If they do these things in the green tree, what will happen in the dry?"

23:34 Jesus . . . doing. Some Greek copies do not have this part of verse 34.

36 Even the soldiers made fun of him. They came to Jesus and offered him some vinegar. 37 They said,

"If you are the king of the Jews, save yourself!"

38 (At the top of the cross these words were written: "THIS IS THE KING OF THE JEWS.") 39 One of the criminals began to shout insults at Jesus:

"Aren't you the Christ? Then save yourself! And save us too!"

40 But the other criminal stopped him. He said,

"You should fear God! You are getting the same punishment as he is. 41 We are punished justly; we should die. But this man has done nothing wrong!"

42 Then this criminal said to Jesus,

"Jesus, remember me when you come into your kingdom!"

43 Then Jesus said to him,

"Listen! What I say is true: Today you will be with me in paradise!"[n]

Jesus Dies

44 It was about noon, and the whole land became dark until three o'clock in the afternoon. 45 There was no sun!

23:43 paradise A place where good people go when they die.

109

The curtain in the Temple[n] was torn into two pieces.

46 Jesus cried out in a loud voice,

"Father, I give you my life."

After Jesus said this, he died. 47 The army officer there saw what happened. He praised God, saying,

"I know this was a good man!"

48 Many people had gathered there to watch this thing. When they saw what happened, they returned home. They beat their chests because they were so sad. 49 Those who were close friends of Jesus were there. Some were women who had followed Jesus from Galilee. They all stood far away from the cross and watched.

Joseph of Arimathea

50-51 A man from the Jewish town of Arimathea was there, too. His name was Joseph. He was a good, religious man. He wanted the kingdom of God to come. Joseph was a member of the Jewish council, but he had not agreed when the other leaders decided to kill Jesus.

52 Joseph went to Pilate to ask for the body of Jesus. 53 So Joseph took the body down from the cross and wrapped it in cloth. Then he put Jesus' body in a tomb that was cut in a wall of rock. This tomb had never been used before.

23:45 curtain in the Temple A curtain divided the Most Holy Place from the other part of the Temple. This was the special building in Jerusalem where God commanded the Jews to worship him.

54 This was late on Preparation[d] Day. When the sun went down, the Sabbath[d] day would begin. 55 The women who had come from Galilee with Jesus followed Joseph. They saw the tomb and saw inside where the body of Jesus was laid.

56 Then the women left to prepare perfumes and spices. On the Sabbath day they rested, as the law of Moses commanded.

Chapter 24

Jesus Rises from Death

1 Very early on the first day of the week, the women came to the tomb where Jesus' body was laid. They brought the spices they had prepared.

2 They found that the stone had been rolled away from the entrance of the tomb. 3 They went in, but they did not find the body of the Lord Jesus.

"Why are you looking for a living person here? This is a place for the dead. 6 Jesus is not here. He has risen from death! Do you remember what he said in Galilee? 7 He said that the Son of Man[d] must be given to evil men, be killed on a cross, and rise from death on the third day."

4 While they were wondering about this, two men in shining clothes suddenly stood beside them. 5 The women were very afraid; they bowed their heads to the ground. The men said to the women,

8 Then the women remembered what Jesus had said.
9 The women left the tomb and told all these things to the 11 apostles[d] and the other followers. 10 These women were Mary Magdalene, Joanna, Mary the mother of James, and some other women. The women told the apostles everything that had happened at the tomb. 11 But they did not believe the women. It sounded like nonsense.

12 But Peter got up and ran to the tomb. He looked in, but he saw only the cloth that Jesus' body had been wrapped in.

Peter went away to be alone, wondering about what had happened.

On the Road to Emmaus

13 That same day two of Jesus' followers were going to a town named Emmaus. It is about seven miles from Jerusalem. 14 They were talking about everything that had happened. 15 While they were discussing these things, Jesus himself came near and began walking with them.

16 (They were not allowed to recognize Jesus.)
17 Then he said,

"What are these things you are talking about while you walk?"

The two followers stopped. Their faces were very sad.

18 The one named Cleopas answered,

"You must be the only one in Jerusalem who does not know what just happened there."

19 Jesus said to them,

"What are you talking about?"

The followers said,

"It is about Jesus of Nazareth. He was a prophet[d] from God to all the people. He said and did many powerful things. 20 Our leaders and the leading priests gave him up to be judged and killed. They nailed him to a cross. 21 But we were hoping that he would free the Jews.

It is now the third day since this happened. 22 And today some women among us told us some amazing things. Early this morning they went to the tomb, 23 but they did not find his body there. They came and told us that they had seen a vision of angels. The angels said that Jesus was alive!

24 So some of our group went to the tomb, too. They found it just as the women said, but they did not see Jesus."

25 Then Jesus said to them,

"You are foolish and slow to realize what is true. You should believe everything the prophets said. 26 They said that the Christ[d] must suffer these things before he enters his glory."

27 Then Jesus began to explain everything that had been written about himself in the Scriptures.[d] He started with Moses, and then he talked about what all the prophets had said about him. 28 They came near the town of Emmaus, and Jesus acted as if he did not plan to stop there.

29 But they begged him,

"Stay with us. It is late; it is almost night."

So he went in to stay with them. 30 Jesus sat down with them and took some bread. He gave thanks for the food and divided it. Then he gave it to them. 31 And then, they were allowed to recognize Jesus.

But when they saw who he was, he disappeared. 32 They said to each other,

"When Jesus talked to us on the road, it felt like a fire burning in us. It was exciting when he explained the true meaning of the Scriptures."

33 So the two followers got up at once and went back to Jerusalem. There they found the 11 apostles[d] and others gathered.

34 They were saying,

"The Lord really has risen from death! He showed himself to Simon."

35 Then the two followers told what had happened on the road. They talked about how they recognized Jesus when he divided the bread.

Jesus Appears to His Followers

36 While the two followers were telling this, Jesus himself stood among those gathered. He said to them,

"Peace be with you."

37 They were fearful and terrified. They thought they were seeing a ghost. 38 But Jesus said,

"Why are you troubled? Why do you doubt what you see? 39 Look at my hands and my feet. It is I myself! Touch me. You can see that I have a living body; a ghost does not have a body like this."

40 After Jesus said this, he showed them his hands and feet.

41 The followers were amazed and very happy. They still could not believe it. Jesus said to them,

"Do you have any food here?"

42 They gave him a piece of cooked fish. 43 While the followers watched, Jesus took the fish and ate it.

44 He said to them,

"Remember when I was with you before? I said that everything written about me must happen—everything in the law of Moses, the books of the prophets,[d] and the Psalms."

45 Then Jesus opened their minds so they could understand the Scriptures.[d]
46 He said to them,

"It is written that the Christ[d] would be killed and rise from death on the third day.
47-48 You saw these things happen—you are witnesses. You must tell people to change their hearts and lives. If they do this, their sins will be forgiven. You must start at Jerusalem and preach these things in my name to all nations.
49 Listen! My Father has promised you something; I will send it to you. But you must stay in Jerusalem until you have received that power from heaven."

Jesus Goes Back to Heaven

50 Jesus led his followers out of Jerusalem almost to Bethany. He raised his hands and blessed them. 51 While he was blessing them, he was separated from them and carried into heaven.

52 They worshiped him and then went back to the city very happy. 53 They stayed in the Temple[d] all the time, praising God.

People and Situations
I Want to Pray For

_____   _____
_____   _____
_____   _____
_____   _____
_____   _____
_____   _____
_____   _____
_____   _____
_____   _____
_____   _____
_____   _____
_____   _____
_____   _____
_____   _____
_____   _____
_____   _____
_____   _____
_____   _____
_____   _____